My DIY

The Stylin' Girl's Guide to D[...]
from Sassy Crafts [...]

Kimberly Potts

Adams Media
Avon, Massachusetts

Published by Adams Media,
an F+W Publications Company
57 Littlefield Street, Avon, MA 02322. U.S.A.
www.adamsmedia.com

ISBN: 1-59337-283-3

Printed in Canada.

J I H G F E D C B A

Library of Congress Cataloging-in-Publication Data
Potts, Kimberly.
My DIY / Kimberly Potts.
p. cm.
ISBN 1-59337-283-3
1. Handicraft for girls—Juvenile literature. I. Title.
TT171.P68 2005
745.5—dc22 2004026847

This publication is designed to provide accurate and authoritative
information with regard to the subject matter covered. It is sold with
the understanding that the publisher is not engaged in rendering legal,
accounting, or other professional advice. If legal advice or other expert
assistance is required, the services of a competent professional person
should be sought.
—From a *Declaration of Principles* jointly adopted by a
Committee of the American Bar Association and a
Committee of Publishers and Associations

Many of the designations used by manufacturers and sellers to distin-
guish their products are claimed as trademarks. Where those designations appear in this book and Adams Media was aware of a trademark
claim, the designations have been printed with initial capital letters.

This book is available at quantity discounts for bulk purchases.
For information, please call 1-800-872-5627.

Dedication

To my hubby John

Thank You's

To my agent June Clark and my editor Danielle Chiotti, for also being excited about eight ways to recycle old T-shirts, and to Jen Mroczka and Christine Chan, my fellow DIY enthusiasts, who provided much support and inspiration. Christine, the bubble-wrap bag goes in the next edition!

Contents

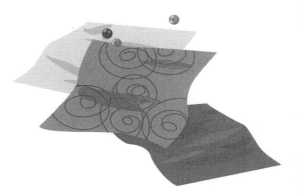

Introduction

So, you, too, are a devotee of the DIY way of life? Well, welcome, crafty girl! This book was written with you in mind, with idea-packed pages of projects, tips, tricks, and recipes that, hopefully, will inspire you to whip up something homemade and fabulous every day!

Okay, so you probably won't craft a new bag for yourself every day or make a special scrapbook for your best friend every day or cook up a big batch of DIY gummi candies every day. But living the DIY lifestyle isn't just about big projects—it's about attitude!

If you're a DIY girl, you probably

❀ . . . know that little things truly do mean a lot. It's not about how much something costs. You can pay big bucks for designer clothing that looks just like the designer clothing someone else paid big bucks for. Or you can showcase your creativity and personality by playing makeover on your own clothes or sprucing up some inexpensive new ones. And when it comes to gifts, DIY fans know that the thought, time, and effort you spend on making something special for someone special far outweighs any present you can buy!

❀ . . . have seen an expensive item in a store and thought, "I could make that myself, for much less money!" and figured out just how to do it!

❀ . . . have an appreciation for the design and reusability of simple things. You finish a box of cereal and wonder what cool things you could do with the empty box. You have a stack of empty mint tins that you're just itching to remake into something handy. You have a stack of old T-shirts you can't bear to throw away, because you just *know* you could make them over into something wonderful and fashionable!

And if you are such a girl, you're in luck: *My DIY* is just for you! In this book, you will find hundreds—really, hundreds!—of ways to create inexpensive and designer-quality clothes and thoughtful and unique gifts, to make DIY versions of store-bought goodies, and to remake everything from old jeans and T-shirts to those promo CDs and old greeting cards into something fabulous!

But before you dive in, just a few quick tips:

❀ Most of the projects in the book require just the most basic of skills. But if you don't already know how to sew, how to use a sewing machine, how to knit, and other crafty skills, ask a friend or family member to teach you, or cruise the "How Do I . . . ?" section on the next few pages for resources on where you can find great (and free!) tutorials on adding to your bag of crafty tricks!

❀ Each project is rated according to ease. There are three degrees of difficulty: "Easy" means you should be able to complete the project with little or no assistance; "Moderate" means you may need the help of a parent, adult, or friend to gather supplies or finish the project; and "Involved" means you should ask your parents or another adult to help you.

❀ Be careful. Ask for permission or help when using a tool or product you've never used before or when doing something in the kitchen you've never done before.

❀ Recycling old things into new, useful ones is one of the main rules of DIY-ing. But always ask permission before raiding Dad's closet for old neckties and T-shirts!

❀ Before beginning any DIY project, always read the entire set of instructions and the materials list, so you can gather all your supplies before you begin. Also, you may have ideas of your own and want to add something to the mix!

You never know when the mood to craft will strike . . . so in Chapter 6 you'll find handy DIY-a-Day calendars—yep, there's one for every month—ensuring that you have an idea for something to do, make, read, or learn every single day of the year! There are also beauty tips, gift ideas, and recipes, as well as the birthstone, flower, and astrological sign for each month (all included to inspire more ideas for gifts and projects) . . . cool, huh?

So start flipping through the *My DIY* pages, gather your supplies, and get ready to make something terrific!

How Do I . . . ?: Terrific Web Sites for Step-by-Step Instructions on Basic Crafting Techniques

Do you know how to sew on a button, fashion a cool rose out of ribbon, or paint a room? These things all seem like simple skills— and they definitely *are* simple, with practice—but they're also skills that can make all the difference in just how far you can take your DIY aspirations! Check out these Web sites and decide which crafty techniques you'd like to master!

Basic Sewing Techniques

The excellent Web site *www.eHow.com* offers instructions on how to thread a needle and prepare to sew, how to sew on a button, how to add a zipper to a sewing project, and how to hem your pants, among dozens of basic and specific sewing tutorials. Just type the topic into the Search box, click the "Search eHow.com" button, and hit "Enter." Voila!

Knitting

About.com offers information on just about everything, including knitting. Go to *www.knitting.about.com* to find lessons for beginning and experienced knitters. These include how to do basic knitting stitches, how to understand knitting patterns, and how to choose knitting supplies. The site also offers free online video demonstrations on how to knit, which can be invaluable to new knitters! P.S.—Once you've mastered the basic stitches, be sure to surf on over to *www.knittingonthenet.com* to get free patterns for dozens of knitting projects!

Crocheting

What's the difference between knitting and crocheting? Is one easier than the other? Each craft has its fans, although a lot of people do feel crocheting is easier to learn than knitting. Check it out for yourself at *www.crochet.about.com*, where you'll find step-by-step instructions on how to crochet a basic chain of stitches and how to join your crocheted pieces. You'll also find free patterns for making your own projects.

Embroidering

Embroidering is an amazing, and easy to learn, skill that will let you turn plain fabrics into truly personal treasures with inexpensive colored threads and a needle. Go to www.yesterdayscharm.com and click the "Embroidery Lessons" link. You'll find a great guide to making various embroidery stitches (with photos!). Also, *www.eHow.com* offers a lesson on how to choose embroidery supplies. (Just type "how to buy embroidery" into the Search box, click the "Search eHow.com" button, and hit "Enter".) Another good site is *www.embroiderybayou. com*, which offers a collection of free patterns to get you started!

Ribbon Roses

Ribbon roses can transform plain T-shirts, tote bags, sheets, curtains, cards, boxes and bags, and countless other plain items into real gems and great gifts! Go to *www.save-on-crafts.com* and search for "ribbon rose" to find a simple, step-by-step lesson on how to make them.

Quilling

Quilling is the art of rolling strips of paper into various shapes, which can then be put together to form very cool designs! You can buy a special quilling tool, but all you really need to get started is some paper, scissors, glue, and a pencil (which fills in nicely for the quilling tool if you don't have one). At *www.crafterscommunity. com*, you'll find a how-to on quilling, along with a guide to basic quilling shapes (just do a search for "quilling"). The CardInspirations Web site offers dozens of quilling projects ideas (at the Web page *www.cardinspirations-usa.com/demo/demo11.htm*), including a Flower Pot Card (*www.cardinspirations-usa.com/demo/quil2.htm*) that you'll want to make for everyone you know!

Make Tassels

Tassels can dress up everything from curtains, pillows, and blankets to bags, bookmarks, and Christmas trees! The Web site *www.iVillage.com* has instructions for making a simple pillow tassel—just type "simple pillow tassel" into the Search box, click "Search iVillage," and hit "Enter"! You can adapt it to make tassels of various sizes, colors, and materials. At *www.eHow.com*, you'll even find instructions on how to make a babydoll out of a tassel. Just type "make a tassel doll" into the Search box, click the "Search eHow.com" button, and hit "Enter."

Make a Pom-Pom

Like tassels, pom-poms are a great accessory to spruce up curtains, curtain rods, tiebacks, lamp shades, bedspreads, socks, shirts, jeans, belts, hats, and scarves. The Web site *www.kid-craft-central.com* has an easy lesson, with photos, on how to make these fun embellishments. Just click the "Arts and Crafts" link, and pom-pom away!

Paint a Room

Even the most experienced home designers agree—the fastest, cheapest way to make over any room is to paint it a new color. At *www.eHow.com*, you'll find a tutorial on every aspect of painting. Type any of the following requests into the Search box, click the "Search eHow.com" button, and hit "Enter" to find cool info on any of the following:

Choose paint
Choose paint color
Prepare a room for painting
How to begin painting

Take the Perfect Picture

Again, it's *www.eHow.com* to the rescue! Type your request into the Search box, click the "Search eHow.com" button, and hit "Enter" to find information on any of the following topics:

Taking digital photos outdoors
Taking digital photos indoors
How to frame a photo shot
How to take good travel photos
How to take good group photos
How to take good portrait photos

As you've probably noticed, *www.eHow.com* offers a wealth of great information for clever crafters. Spend a few minutes surfing the site's list of tutorials, and you might just find a whole new hobby! Other great Web sites for general crafting how-to's include *www. essortment.com*, *www.diynet.com*, and *www.familyfun.go.com*.

The DIY Toolbox: Supplies Every DIY Girl Should Have for When the Mood to Craft Strikes

If you have even a few of these materials around the house, you're all set to make something special! About that toolbox . . . you can buy a fancy, expensive "craft box," but for a sturdier, cheaper idea, try an actual toolbox for storing your craft goodies! Available in discount stores, hardware stores, home improvement centers (or maybe even your own garage!), real toolboxes usually have many compartments, secure latches, and, again, are super sturdy! Things you should always keep on hand include these:

* Magazines or catalogs
* Clear tape
* Markers, crayons, colored pencils, regular pencils with erasers, gel pens, watercolors, and art paints
* Scissors
* Ribbon in any and every size, shape, length, color, and type
* Fabric scraps
* Felt
* Needles and thread
* Yarn
* Glue of various types—fabric glue, wood glue, glue stick, spray adhesive, glue gun, and glue sticks

- Glitter
- Rhinestones
- Beads
- Paper of every size, shape, color, and texture
- Clip art
- Stencils
- Tissue paper
- Magnetic backing
- Fabric trims
- Various empty and clean jars, bottles, cans, containers, and boxes
- Jewelry-making supplies, like earring wires, jewelry cord, pin backs, and barrette backings
- Paintbrushes
- Pipe cleaners
- Stickers
- Hole punchers of various shapes and sizes
- Rubber stamps and inks
- Buttons
- Embroidery threads
- Popsicle sticks
- Silk flowers
- Sequins
- Candle-making supplies (candle wax, wicks, small votive holders, etc.)
- Craft wire
- Essential oils
- Cheap, plain photo frames
- Craft foam
- Pom-poms
- Jingle bells
- Plain, inexpensive journals
- Plain, inexpensive photo albums
- Spray paint
- Clay
- Newspaper (especially those colorful Sunday comics!)
- Paper mache boxes and shapes

- Baskets in various sizes, shapes, and colors
- Zip-closure bags
- Tweezers
- A good, strong ruler (metal is best)
- Baby wipes (great for cleaning up after a craft project!)

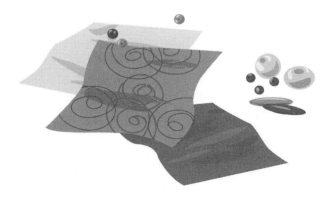

1

My DIY Room!

Besides school, you probably spend more of your time in your bedroom than anywhere else, right? So, of course, you want your room to be comfy and cool, and it has to reflect your personality. This chapter is full of projects and ideas to turn your room into your sanctuary, where you feel comfortable studying, hanging out with friends, sleeping, and, natch, creating all your DIY concoctions!

Aloha, Shirt, Aloha, Pillow!

In Hawaiian, *Aloha* means both "hello" and "goodbye." For this project, you're saying goodbye to an old Hawaiian shirt and hello to a festive new pillow for your room or for getting comfy in the family room while you're watching TV! Don't worry if you don't have an old shirt to recycle. Hawaiian shirts are a great vintage and thrift-store find. Or maybe you can ask your dad for permission to raid his closet!

Project difficulty: Moderate

Materials

Hawaiian shirt, any size

Fiberfill (a stuffing material that is available at any craft store)

Thread to match the shirt

Tools U Need

Sewing needle

Scissors

Iron

DIY Step-by-Step:

1. Button the shirt and iron it. Turn it wrong side out, and sew the armholes closed.
2. Sew the bottom of the shirt closed.
3. Now turn the shirt right side out. Begin stuffing it through the neck hole. Make sure you fill the arms. Keep going until the entire pillow is full up to the neck opening.
4. Press the neck down flat, so the opening is closed. Flip the collar up, and sew straight across so the hole is closed. Flip the collar back down again, and now you've got a cool pillow!

Extra touch: Hot-glue or sew a lei around the "neck" of the pillow!

Bloomin' Bulletin Board

This bulletin board will be a great place to keep all your messages, important reminders, and photos. It looks so pretty that you may want to make one for a friend, too!

Project difficulty: Easy

Materials

1 plain corkboard bulletin board

1 yard of artificial turf (available at hobby and home improvement stores)

Several large artificial flowers, of various types and colors (available at any craft or discount store, and cheaper when you buy them in a bunch and cut them apart yourself)

10 pushpins

Tools U Need

Glue gun and glue sticks or other strong glue (like e6000, a brand available at any craft or home improvement store)

Tape measure or yardstick

Scissors

DIY Step-by-Step:

1. Measure the inside of the bulletin board (the actual cork part, where you will pin things). Cut a piece of the artificial turf to that exact size. Glue it to the bulletin board, and let the glue dry.
2. Cut the stems off all the flowers, leaving each one with a flat back. Glue each one to the top of a pushpin, and let the glue dry.
3. Hang your grassy bulletin board, and use your new flower pushpins to decorate your hanging yard!

Extra touch: If you don't want to buy fake flowers, make paper flowers and use them for the pushpins.

Un-Boring Board Game Art

Un-Boring Board Game Art is the perfect way to turn an old game into a fresh and unique decoration for your room! Just take an old edition of Scrabble, Monopoly, or Candy Land and some hot glue and the game's on . . . on your wall, that is!

Project difficulty: Moderate

Materials

Board game (an old one you have at home, or an inexpensive one from a yard sale, vintage shop, or secondhand store. Don't worry if a few pieces are missing . . . you'll still be able to design a master-piece!)

Large sheet of sturdy foamboard

Frame or art hanging kit (available at any craft, hardware, home improvement, or general discount retailer store)

Tools U Need

Glue gun and glue sticks, or other strong glue

Scissors

Tape measure or yardstick

DIY Step-by-Step:

1 Measure the actual board part of the game, and cut a piece of foamboard to that exact size. Glue the game board to the foam-board, and let the glue dry.

2 Arrange the game pieces on the game board any way you like them. Glue them down securely. Here are a few tips for display-ing the pieces. Fan out Monopoly money and glue it down; spell out your name or a favorite quote with Scrabble letters on the board and glue the whole thing down; display the game pieces in a way that makes it appear a game is in progress.

③ Following the directions on the frame or the art hanging kit package, attach your art or frame hanging kit to the back of the foamboard and hang it on your wall!

Extra touches: If you're using a Scrabble game, spell out the names of all your family members with the tiles, and glue those to the board. It'll make a great piece of art for your family room or even for the kitchen! Another idea is to use a Trouble game (you know, the game with the "pop-o-matic" action?)—and hang it on your bedroom door. When someone wants to enter your room, she doesn't have to knock . . . she just has to push the popper!

Le Chandelier de Plastic Cups

Yep, it may sound fancy, and it definitely looks fancy when you're finished—which is why no one will believe that a cheapo strand of Christmas lights and a package of plastic picnic cups can be turned into something so cool and sparkly. But it can . . . and it makes the perfect chandelier-like centerpiece to hang from your ceiling!

Project difficulty: Moderate

Materials

50 disposable plastic cups (the Solo brand cups are great, and clear ones work best—you will have leftovers, but it's good to make sure you have around 50 because the number of cups it takes to form the chandelier depends on the size of the cups)

1 string of Christmas lights with approximately 35 bulbs, either colored or white (see the Extra touch at the end to make this decision)

Tools U Need

Glue gun and glue sticks, or other strong glue

Strong fishing line

A woodworking awl, ice pick, or other item to punch holes in plastic

DIY Step-by-Step:

1. Start by punching a small hole in the middle of the bottom of one cup. Try inserting a strand of Christmas lights through the hole. The hole has to be big enough for the lights to pass through, but not so big that they'll fall out again. When you've determined what size hole works best, make a hole of that size in the middle of the bottoms of all 50 cups.

2. Begin gluing the cups together. Put glue on one side of one cup, and stick it to another cup. Keep the cups even at the top and bottom. Add another cup in a line with the first two. Do the same thing with another cup. Continue gluing the cups together, side by side. They will begin to curve around in a circular shape, forming a ball-like structure.

3. Once you have glued enough cups together to form a half-circle (the structure should look like half of a ball at this point), set them aside. Let the glue fully dry so the cups are tightly secured to each other.

4. While the first half-circle is drying, repeat the process of gluing two cups together, side by side, and adding cups to the first two, until you have another half-circle. Let this semicircle dry thoroughly also.

5. Once the first semicircle is dry, take your strand of Christmas lights and begin inserting the bulbs into the holes you've made. Insert one bulb into the bottom of each cup. Count the number of cups you have used in total (for both half-circles). Most Christmas lights have about 35 lights. If you used more than 35 cups, just skip one randomly every now and then.

6. The glue on the second half-circle should now be dry. Place it beside the first half-circle, and continue inserting lights into the bottoms of the cups, one bulb to a cup. Again, remember to skip one here or there if you've used more than 35 cups in total.

7. Once all the lights have been inserted into the cups, carefully fit the two half-circles together. Another pair of hands would be very helpful here. IMPORTANT: Let the end of the strand of lights (where the plug is) dangle down on the inside of the cups, where the two half-circles fit together. This way, the cord will

hang free and let you easily plug in your chandelier. Then glue the two half-circles together.

8. Once the two halves are glued together, set the whole piece aside and let it dry and set. When you're sure it's secure, punch a hole in one cup on each opposite side of the sphere—you only need to do this to two cups. Take two long pieces of fishing line and tie each one very securely through each hole. Join the two pieces of fishing line together at the top and tie them securely together there.

9. Now you're ready to plug in and hang your spectacular new chandelier!

Extra touch: Clear cups with colored Christmas lights will look spectacular, but if you're trying to keep a theme going with a certain color in your room, try finding plastic cups in that color, and use a strand of white Christmas lights inside the chandelier!

A Dresser Dress

Your dresser holds all your pretty clothes, so why shouldn't it get a little garment to make it look pretty, too?

Project difficulty: Moderate

Materials

Piece of pretty fabric roughly twice as big as the top of your dresser (or plain fabric that you will dress up—you can also use an old sheet or towel or other fabric scrap, as long as it's big enough)

Fabric trim (such as pom-poms, tassels, ribbons, and so on)

Matching thread

Tools U Need

Sewing needle or fabric glue

Scissors

An iron

Measuring tape

DIY Step-by-Step:

1. Measure the length and width of the top of your dresser. Take that measurement and add at least two inches to all four sides. For example, if your dresser is 24 inches across and 18 inches from front to back, the measurement for your dresser dress would be 26 inches × 20 inches. Cut the piece of fabric to that size, making sure the material is not so long that it covers your drawers.

2. Using a needle and thread or fabric glue, make a ¼-inch hem all the way around the piece of fabric. Once the hem is made, press it into place with an iron.

3. Sew or use fabric glue to add a decorative trim all the way around the fabric.

4. Dress your dresser!

Extra touch: Using embroidery stitches or fabric paint, write your name across the dresser dress or add extra designs to the edges of the fabric, since they are the part that will be most visible on your dresser.

Bed Curtains

Curtains? For your bed? Yep, this elegant treatment, which is oh-so-easy to make, will make your sleep space something special!

Project difficulty: Moderate

Materials

Curtain rod or two, if necessary, at least the width/length of your bed

A pretty set of curtains, or a plain piece of gauzy fabric (you could also recycle a pretty bed sheet for this project). Fabric should be as wide as the curtain rod and long enough to reach the floor when the curtain rod is hung.

Curtain hooks, shower-curtain hooks, clothespins, or pieces of ribbon—for holding curtains to curtain rod

2 pieces of ribbon, garland, fabric trim, tassels, or string of beads that you can use as curtain tiebacks

2 pushpins

Tools U Need

Tools for installing the curtain rod, as described on the package

DIY Step-by-Step:

1. Install the curtain rod above your bed according to the curtain rod instructions. Place it as far below the ceiling as you would like, but a good spot is at least a foot or so below the ceiling. (Be sure to ask for help if any power tools or complex measurements are involved.)

2. If you're using premade curtain panels, hang them from the rod. If you're making your own curtains, cut your fabric in half from top to bottom. Sew or fabric glue a small hem at the bottom. Make a hem at the top that is big enough to accommodate the curtain rod.

3. Once the bed curtains are hung, pull one panel to each side and secure it to the wall with a "tieback" that you will secure to the wall with a pushpin. Ideas for tiebacks include pieces of ribbon, Christmas tree garland, fabric trim like pom-poms, scarves, stringed beads, and so on.

Extra touch: Add a valance to your bed curtains! Just take some extra fabric—like a matching scrap of fabric from another project or a pretty, inexpensive sheet—and drape it over each end of the curtain rod, making it sway a bit in the middle.

Raise the Curtain: Funky Touches for Your Window Treatments

Anyone can thread a piece of fabric onto a curtain rod, right? But these special, yet oh-so-simple, ideas will make your window look more like a piece of art than a big hole in the wall! Take a look at the following instructions, and then make your choice.

Project difficulty: Easy to Moderate

Materials

Just about anything you think would look cool decorating your window (including fabric, lengths of ribbon or cord, decorative elements such as buttons, and so on)

Tools U Need

Depends on the materials and techniques you choose—have your toolbox handy!

DIY Step-by-Step

1. To create interesting tiebacks for your curtains, use ribbons, hair accessories, or old costume jewelry—all things you can find at flea markets and yard sales!

2. To make a new kind of curtain, cut and tie long lengths of ribbon all the way across a curtain rod (you can tie the ribbon directly to the rod, or attach them with a strong glue), and then tie them back as you would curtain panels.

3. To spruce up a plain sheer curtain panel, sew or hot-glue various buttons or small ribbon bows all over it.

4. To light up your curtain rod, wrap a strand of Christmas lights around your curtain rod! You can also paint or decoupage Styrofoam balls and put them at each end of your curtain rods as finials. For extra sparkle, add glitter or beads after you paint them.

⑤ To change the look of your curtain hooks, hang your curtains from the rod by using wooden clothespins. You could even paint the clothespins to match the colors in the rest of your room! You can also tie your curtains to the curtain rod with pieces of wide ribbon that coordinates with the color of the curtains.

⑥ To make your own personal expression, buy plain bamboo shades and paint your own funky designs on them! Or use the tie-dye technique to color a white sheet and use it as a curtain! The Rit dye company's Web site has complete instructions on how to tie-dye (*www.ritdye.com*).

Color Your World: Great Color Combinations for Decorating Your Room

Some paint, a few pillows, a new rug, a panel of curtains . . . but what colors will make your room pop with style and your personality? Consider these color combos, and various shades of them, and decide which hues will help you create your perfect bedroom sanctuary:

- ✿ Blue and green
- ✿ Blue, green, and yellow
- ✿ Red and pink
- ✿ Pink and orange
- ✿ Pink and brown
- ✿ Pink, yellow, and orange
- ✿ Pink and green
- ✿ Pink and black (very retro!)
- ✿ A dark or bright shade of pink and a very light shade of pink
- ✿ A dark or bright shade of green and a very light shade of green
- ✿ Lavender and green
- ✿ Black and white (always a classic color combo!)
- ✿ Red and black
- ✿ Red and white
- ✿ Light blue and light purple

Erasable Lap Desk

Sometimes you just don't feel like studying at a desk, right? With this portable workspace, you can get work done on your bed, on the floor, on the couch . . . even outside!

Project difficulty: Easy

Materials

Dry-erase board, any size you want

Pillow the same size as or a little bigger than the dry-erase board

Pillowcase, or piece of fabric at least twice as big as the pillow

Tools U Need

Needle and thread, or fabric glue

Glue gun and glue sticks, or other strong glue

Dry-erase marker(s) and eraser

DIY Step-by-Step:

1. Put the pillowcase on your pillow. If using fabric, fold in half with wrong side out. Sew or glue edges together, leaving one side open. Turn right side out, and fit over pillow. For homemade cover or pillowcase, sew or use fabric glue to close the opening.
2. Cover the back of the dry-erase board with a heavy layer of glue, spread evenly and entirely across. Center the board over the pillow and press firmly to join them together.
3. Let the glue between pillow and board dry thoroughly.
4. Get to work, with your new Erasable Lap Desk!

Extra touches: Instead of a readymade pillow, you could also use a thick piece of foam covered with fabric instead. If you have an old pair of jeans you plan to recycle, take one of the back pockets and glue it to the pillow side of your desk. This makes a great place to store your dry-erase markers and eraser!

A Garden-Variety Headboard

With a little help installing this simple headboard, and a little imagination afterwards, you can have a very inexpensive headboard that will look like a million bucks and make you feel like you're waking up in a garden every morning!

Project difficulty: Involved

Materials

Picket fence or garden trellis (both available at any home improvement store) in one or several sections that add up to the same width as your bed

Paint and a paintbrush

Fake flowers, butterflies, and ivy (available at any craft store)

Tools U Need

Hardware to secure the headboard to the wall (nails, anchors, screws, etc.) and hammer or drill, as appropriate

Glue gun and glue sticks, or other strong glue

DIY Step-by-Step:

1. If the fencing or trellis is unfinished, paint it. (You can usually find these pieces already painted, which will save a lot of time.) White will look great in almost any room, especially after you've decorated the wood, but you could also paint the headboard to match other colors in your room.

2. Ask for help from a handy family member or friend to attach the fencing or trellis to the wall right above your bed. The trellis must be fixed securely to the wall with whatever hardware is appropriate, like sturdy screws drilled into the wall studs. IMPORTANT: Make sure the fencing or trellis is completely secure! You don't want a big piece of wood falling down on you in the middle of the night!

③ Now for the fun part! Arrange your fake flowers, butterflies, and ivy all across the headboard, and glue the pieces down. Some of the flowers may have wire in them, which you can also use to secure them to the headboard. Weave the ivy in and out, gather flowers in small bunches across the board, and place butterflies here and there!

Extra touches: Paint two small, unfinished birdhouses in colors that match the rest of your room, and mount one on each side of the bed, right above the Garden-Variety Headboard. Find a small mailbox, paint it to match your headboard or some of the lovely flowers on the headboard, and secure it to the wall, next to the bed. It's perfect for storing your mail or your magazines!

Candy-Wrapper Art

You've heard of pop art? How about *lolli*-pop art? The idea of this fun art project is to pick one of your favorite candy wrappers and make a collage by repeating the pattern of the wrapper.

Project difficulty: Easy

Materials

Large piece of foamboard (any size)

Several dozen of your favorite candy wrappers (as many as it will take to cover the foamboard). Here are some that make a color-ful pattern: Starburst fruit chews (use all the different colors), Blow Pops, Tootsie Rolls or Tootsie Roll Pops, Dum Dum lollipops, Her-shey's Miniatures candy bars, Life Savers, Pop Rocks, and M&M's.

Decoupage glue (available at any craft store) or regular white glue (like Elmer's)

Tools U Need

Craft paintbrush

DIY Step-by-Step:

1. Paint the backs of the wrappers with decoupage or Elmer's glue, and arrange them on the foamboard. Arranging them simply, side by side until they form a row, then continuing the rows until the board is completely covered, makes a cool design.
2. Once the board is covered with wrappers, "seal" the decoupage by painting the entire surface with a thin layer of glue. The glue will dry clear, with a shiny finish.
3. Hang your masterpiece!

Extra touch: Make several pieces of candy-wrapper art (either with the same kind of wrapper or a mix of different ones) and group them together for a eye-catching display!

Photo Cube Bookends

These groovy decorations not only make use of your old CD cases, they also show off your favorite photos and make cool bookends for your shelves . . . it's a DIY triple crown!

Project difficulty: Easy

Materials

4 old or promo CDs
4 empty, clear CD cases
4 photos (or 8, if you also want to display photos in the backs of the cases). For fronts, cut photos to 4.75 × 4.75 inch squares; for backs, cut photos to 5.5 × 4.75 inches.

Tools U Need

Glue gun and glue sticks, or other strong glue
Scissors
Ruler

DIY Step-by-Step:

1. Remove any labels or CD booklets from the CD cases. If the CD is old and you don't want it anymore, leave it in there. Otherwise, replace it with a giveaway CD, like those from AOL or other promos. Keeping a CD in the case gives it some added weight and makes the bookend sturdier. If you plan on displaying photos in the back part of the case, cut those to size and put them in now.

2. Stand the CD cases up and form a square with them, with the front of each case (the part that opens) facing outward.

3. Carefully glue the edges together, making sure the cases overlap enough to adhere to each other, but not so much that the case is blocked and unable to open. You should have a square with cases that, once they are permanently glued together, will still open. Once you have that arranged and the glue applied, let the glue dry and the square "cement."

4. When the glue is dry and the square is set, cut your photos to size and insert them in the cases. The great thing is that since the cases still open, you can rotate new photos in anytime you like. It's like your own little museum!

Extra touches: If you don't want to cut up your original photos for the project, you could make photocopies before you begin. Also, instead of clear CD cases, you could try colored ones. Instead of personal photos, you could also use magazine cutouts, posters, maps, wrapping paper, scrapbook paper, calendar photos, fabric with a cool pattern, labels, stickers, and other paper goodies to display in your bookends!

2

My DIY Beauty!

Betcha never knew your beauty products could smell and taste this good! Before you go dropping big bucks on some pricey department-store beauty goodies, take a look at these fantastic DIY Beauty projects. You may find that you don't need to go much farther than the refrigerator to whip up something fantastic for your skin, teeth, or hair, or for a refreshing and relaxing bath!

Strawberry-Banana Toothpaste

Is it possible that toothpaste can taste this good? Yep! Just remember . . . even if you're tempted, it's for brushing, not eating!

Project difficulty: Easy

Materials

1 cup baking soda

2 drops strawberry flavoring (food flavorings are available at any baking supply store, in the baking section of a craft store, or online—try *www.candylandcrafts.com*)

2 drops banana flavoring

¼ cup salt

¼ cup water

Tools U Need

Small bowl and spoon

Measuring cup

Airtight container for storing the toothpaste

DIY Step-by-Step:

1. Using a large spoon, mix the baking soda, salt, and water in a small bowl.
2. Once the mix is thoroughly blended, add the flavoring drops, one at a time, until they're blended in well.
3. Store the paste in an airtight container.
4. Spread a small amount of paste across your toothbrush and brush as usual!

Extra touch: Try other flavor combinations for the toothpaste. Some ideas would be banana and orange, strawberry and orange, or vanilla and cherry!

Sweet Tooth: Keep Your Pearly Whites Healthy

You've heard the saying "The world always looks brighter from behind a smile," right? Here are a few tips for making sure your smile is at its brightest!

- ✿ Buy the softest-bristled toothbrush you can find. Bristles that are too hard will break down the enamel on your teeth and damage your gums.
- ✿ After brushing and flossing, and before using mouthwash, try gently scraping your tongue with a spoon (the concave, or open, part pointed down) to ensure fresh breath. This also helps to scrape away some of the germs that build up on your tongue.
- ✿ Don't grip your toothbrush too tightly. That can cause you to brush too hard. Instead, grip it gently, and brush your teeth with firm, but not hard, pressure.
- ✿ Do not move toothbrush up and down. Instead, move it in a circular manner, which is more gentle on your tooth enamel and gums.
- ✿ Most dentists recommend that you brush at least twice a day and floss at least once. Flossing is just as important as brushing, because it helps get rid of food particles and germs that get trapped between your teeth, and which can lead to gum disease . . . blech!

Neapolitan Lip Frosting

Mmmm . . . you know that yummy neapolitan ice cream, the kind that's part vanilla, part chocolate, and part strawberry? That's exactly the idea with this project, which will result in three tasty flavors of lip gloss!

Project difficulty: Easy

Materials

1 jar petroleum jelly

1 small canister Hershey's cocoa powder

1 envelope strawberry Kool-Aid or Jell-O mix

1 small bottle vanilla extract

Tools U Need

3 small to medium microwave-safe bowls

Measuring spoons

3 mixing spoons

DIY Step-by-Step:

1. For the chocolate lip frosting: Stir together 4 tablespoons of petroleum jelly with 4 teaspoons of cocoa powder. Put the mixture in the microwave for 30 seconds. Remove it and stir gently. If the mixture is not melted, cook it for another 30 seconds in the microwave. Check it again and continue this cycle until the mixture has melted and the gloss is formed. Let it cool slightly, and store it in an airtight container.

2. For the strawberry lip frosting: Put 4 tablespoons of petroleum jelly and the packet of strawberry Kool-Aid in a bowl. Cook the mixture in the microwave for 30 seconds. Remove it and stir gently. If the mixture is not melted, cook it for another 30 seconds in the microwave. Check it again and continue this cycle until the mixture has melted and the gloss is formed. Let it cool slightly, and store it in an airtight container.

3. For the vanilla lip frosting: Put 4 tablespoons of petroleum jelly with 3 teaspoons of vanilla extract in a bowl. Put the mixture in the microwave for 30 seconds. Remove it and stir gently. If the mixture is not melted, cook it for another 30 seconds in the microwave. Check it again and continue this cycle until the mixture has melted and the gloss is formed. Let it cool slightly and store it in an airtight container.

4. Apply cooled lip gloss with your finger, or use a cotton swab.

Extra touches: For a cool way to carry all your yummy glosses, take a clean, empty Altoids or other mint tin. Cut small dividers out of cardboard or other stiff paper. Cover these in plastic wrap or clear tape, and use them to divide the tin into three compartments. Put some of each flavor of lip gloss in the tin, make a fun label for it, and your lips will never go un-shiny again!

Sweet-As-Honey Facial Gel

A simple DIY recipe that will leave your skin silky smooth, thanks to the exfoliating effects of honey.

Project difficulty: Easy

Materials

1 cup honey

¼ cup almond oil

¼ cup olive oil (or you can use ½ cup of one of the oils and eliminate the other)

Tools U Need

Bowl and spoon

Measuring cup

Airtight container for storage

DIY Step-by-Step:

1. Using a spoon, stir all the ingredients together in a small bowl. Make sure they're mixed together very well.
2. To use, smooth the gel onto your face, being careful to AVOID THE EYE AREA! Gently massage it into your skin for three minutes.
3. With warm water—not too hot—and a soft washcloth, gently rinse the gel from your face. Once it's removed, rinse your face

again, this time with cool water, and gently pat dry with a clean towel.

4 Extra gel must be stored in the refrigerator, and can be used for up to three weeks.

Extra touch: Store your Sweet-As-Honey Facial Gel in an empty plastic honey bear!

Zit Zappers: DIY Remedies for Those Pesky Pimples!

Try one of these methods for clearing up a pesky pimple with things you probably already have in your home (just make sure you keep all these homemade remedies away from your eyes!):

- ✿ Rub a peeled raw potato on the blemish. Leave the potato juice on the area for 10–15 minutes, and then rinse it off with cool water. The juice helps reduce the swelling and redness of the blemish.
- ✿ Dab a bit of white toothpaste—paste, not the gel kind—on the infected area and leave it on overnight. It will help dry up the blemish.
- ✿ Mix 1 tablespoon of lemon juice with 1 tablespoon of salt. Using a cotton swab or cotton ball, dab a bit of the mixture on the blemish. Let it dry, and repeat. The combo of lemon and salt will help reduce the redness and swelling of the pimple, and will ultimately help dry it up completely!

Creamsicle Bath Sprinkle

What better way to relax than with the creamy, dreamy smell of a tasty orange and vanilla Creamsicle! This bath time treat doesn't just smell great and look pretty, though—the milk powder will also leave your skin cool and smooth. Just like a Creamsicle!

Project difficulty: Easy

Materials

1½ cups powdered milk (available at any supermarket)

1½ cups Epsom salt (in the pharmacy section of your supermarket, or at any drugstore)

½ cup baking soda

2 drops orange essential oil (you'll find a great selection of essential oils online, like at *www.candylandcrafts.com*)

2 drops vanilla essential oil or vanilla extract

2 drops red food coloring

2 drops yellow food coloring

Tools U Need

Small scoop (either a small plastic spoon, or a scoop you recycle from a can of coffee or a box of laundry detergent)

Large mixing bowl and spoon

Measuring cup

Airtight storage container or large zip-closure bag

DIY Step-by-Step:

1. Using the spoon, mix the milk powder, salt, and baking soda together in the bowl.
2. Add the essential oils to the dry mix and stir it all together thoroughly.
3. Stir in 1 drop each of the red and yellow food coloring. If the mixture is not a bright enough orange, put 1 more drop of each color into the mix and stir. Don't use any more food coloring than you need . . . you don't want your skin to turn orange in the bathtub!
4. Store your yummy Creamsicle Bath Sprinkle in an airtight container, and pour one or two scoops under running water each time you fill the tub for a bath!

Extra touch: Store the sprinkle mix in a large salt shaker or in an empty salt box with a pour spout.

Chocolate-Almond Bath Cookies

These extra special bath goodies are so yummy smelling and so cute that you'll have to keep some for yourself, but you'll also want to give some away to friends and family!

Project difficulty: Moderate

Materials

3 cups sea salt

1 cup baking soda

3 eggs

1 cup cornstarch

6 tablespoons corn oil

10 drops chocolate essential oil (*www.candylandcrafts.com* has lots of essential oils)

10 drops almond essential oil

Tools U Need

Large mixing bowl

Small to medium bowl

Large wooden spoon

Measuring cup

Fork or whisk

Baking sheet

Airtight container

DIY Step-by-Step:

1 Preheat your oven to 375 degrees.
2 In the large bowl, beat the eggs together with a fork or a whisk, as if you were making scrambled eggs. Beat in the corn oil and all 20 drops of the essential oils.
3 In the medium bowl, mix together the sea salt, baking soda, and cornstarch.

4. Slowly add the dry ingredients to the egg and oil mixture, about ⅓ of the dry ingredients at a time. Once all the ingredients are mixed together, continue to stir until they are well blended into a cookie-dough consistency.

5. With a large tablespoon, scoop a spoonful of the dough and roll it into a ball. Put the ball on the cookie sheet and lightly press it with the bottom of a glass or with your thumb until it flattens into a cookie shape. Repeat with the rest of the dough.

6. Put the sheet full of bath cookies into the preheated oven and bake for 6–7 minutes. The bath cookies will not turn brown, but they should be firm when you take them out of the oven.

7. Remove the bath cookies from the sheet and set them on a piece of wax paper to cool for a couple of hours.

8. Store them in an airtight container . . . like an old cookie jar! (P.S.: Make sure you label it so your little bro or sis doesn't try to scarf 'em down!)

9. To use, drop a couple of cookies into the water when you're filling up the tub for a relaxing soak. They'll gradually dissolve in the water, releasing all their skin-softening goodness into your bath!

Extra touches: Store the cookies in a cookie tin! Also, if you're going to give them as a gift, package them in a pretty glass jar or a small cookie jar, or make larger bath cookies and individually wrap them in plastic wrap. Make labels with instructions on how to use them, and tie each one with a ribbon.

Bubblin' Bath Jam

What's better than a bubble bath? A bubble bath that smells this good and looks this adorable in the jar!

Project difficulty: Easy

Materials

2 boxes plain, unflavored gelatin (at any supermarket)

1 cup clear liquid soap, like hand soap, dish soap, or baby shampoo

1½ cups water

Small plastic toy, like a rubber ducky, boat, ship, or fish (look in the party favor section of a craft store or party supplies center for something with an aquatic theme)

Blue food coloring

Essential oil—any aroma (blueberry, raspberry, and grape all work well) from a craft supplier like *www.candylandcrafts.com*

Tools U Need

Small scoop (either a small plastic spoon, or a scoop you recycle from a can of coffee or a box of laundry detergent)

Large mixing bowl

Spoon

Measuring cup

Pot for boiling water

Large jar with a lid (like a clean jelly jar!)

DIY Step-by-Step:

1. Heat the water in the pot until it's boiling.
2. Open the boxes of plain gelatin and put them into the mixing bowl. Pour—carefully!—the boiling water into the bowl, and slowly stir it until the gelatin is completely dissolved. Let the mixture cool for 10–15 minutes.
3. Next, stir in the liquid soap and 1 drop of the blue food coloring. If you want the jelly to be slightly brighter, put in 1 more drop, but don't use more than 2. Next, stir in 6 drops of the essential oil.
4. Pour the mixture into the large jar. Put the small toy inside, and push it down to the bottom of the jar. Put the lid on the jar.
5. Put the jar into the refrigerator and let it set for at least 6 hours.
6. To use, drop two or three scoopfuls of jam under the running water when you're filling the tub for a bath!

Extra touches: Combine any color food coloring and flavor of essential oil to come up with your own bath jam creations. Also, remove the labels from recycled jelly or jam jars, design your own label, and give the cool jars as gifts!

Hand-and-Foot "Facial"

Yeah, yeah, facials are for your face. Just as a regular facial rids your face of dead skin and enriches it with ingredients to leave it soft and healthy, a facial for your hands and feet will accomplish the same thing. Plus, it will feel so good!

Project difficulty: Moderate

Materials

4 large plastic sandwich or freezer bags

½ cup sugar

4 tablespoons plain hand lotion

Tools U Need

Heating pad

Measuring cup

Tablespoon

DIY Step-by-Step:

1. Working over the bathroom sink, measure 2 tablespoons of sugar into your hand. Mix just a drop or two of water with the sugar—you don't want the sugar to dissolve.
2. Massage the sugar all over your hands and work it into the skin on both hands for at least a full minute. The sugar exfoliates your skin and helps get rid of dead skin cells.
3. Rinse your hands thoroughly with warm water, making sure to get rid of all the sugar. Dry your hands.

④ Put one tablespoon of hand lotion into the palm of your hand. Smooth it all over your hand, put one of the plastic bags over your hand (covering it completely) and then put your hand under the heating pad on a low setting. Let it stay under the heating pad for 5–10 minutes. It should be very relaxing!

⑤ Turn off the heating pad, remove your hand from the bag, and rinse it thoroughly, with warm water. Doesn't it feel silky soft?

⑥ Repeat on the other hand.

⑦ Repeat the entire process on each of your feet. Beware: The "facial" is even more soothing on your feet. Don't fall asleep!

Extra touch: Invite some friends over and have a Hand-and-Foot "Facial" party!

Good Things Come in Pretty Packages: Presenting Your DIY Beauty Goodies!

You've got the recipes for some delicious beauty treats . . . now all you need is some cool packaging to store them. Ask and you shall receive:

Labels—Make pretty ones on your computer, using cool clip art and funky fonts, and print them out on sticky-back or label paper. Or, on label paper, use markers, glitter, and glue to create a unique label for your beauty goodies. Bonus tip: Give your goodies special names, like Lip Frosting for lip gloss, or Bathball for fizzy bath bombs.

Film containers—Wash them with warm soapy water, design a great label, and use them to package your DIY lip glosses and balms.

Peanut-butter jars—Wash them with warm soapy water and soak the jar to make the label easy to remove. Replace it with your own label, and package your DIY scented powder in it. Bonus tip: Fill the jar a couple of inches to the top. Cut a new sponge in a round shape, small enough to fit inside the jar, for a cool powder puff!

Jelly jars—Wash them thoroughly with warm soapy water and soak the jar to make the label easy to remove. Replace it with your

(continued)

own label and package your homemade bubble bath jelly in it! Bonus tip: Tie a pretty colored plastic spoon to the jar—for scooping the jelly into the bath—with a matching ribbon!

Salt shakers—Scour yard sales, thrift shops, and 99-cent stores for cool salt shakers, or plain ones that you can spruce up with glitter, fabric trim, beads, and other sparkly things. Use the shakers to package your bath salts, adding a little tag tied around the shaker with the name of the product (like Bath Seasonings or Bath Sprinkles).

Plastic ketchup bottle—Find inexpensive new ones at a craft store, baking supply shop, or restaurant supply company, or wash out and remove the label from a small ketchup bottle you have at home. Make a new label for it and use it to package your homemade toothpaste!

Water bottle—Make sure it's the kind with the sip or squirt top. Remove the label, replace it with a label you make and use it to package your DIY bubble bath jam!

Tennis ball canister or Pringles can—Wash out thoroughly, make a special label for the can, and use it to package several homemade bath bombs.

Watercolor palette—You know those plastic, multi-compartment trays that hold several colors of water paints and a paintbrush? If you have an empty, or nearly empty one, thoroughly scrub the entire container with hot, soapy water, making sure every trace of paint is washed from the individual compartments. Make a new label for the lid and fill the compartments with lip gloss! Bonus tip: Use a few different flavors of lip gloss to fill the set, and add a cosmetic brush for "painting" your lips!

Peanut-Butter-Cup Body Frosting

Do you love peanut-butter cups so much that you want to *be* one? All right, maybe not. But it might be pretty cool to smell like one, right? Especially if it's making your skin soft at the same time!

Project difficulty: Easy

Materials

2 cups unscented lotion (an inexpensive purchase at most 99-cent stores, Target, or discount drugstores)

1 bottle chocolate essential oil or flavoring oil (another good find at www.candylandcrafts.com)

1 bottle peanut butter essential oil or flavoring oil

4 vitamin E capsules (also an inexpensive purchase at most 99-cent stores, Target, or discount drugstores)

Tools U Need

Mixing bowl and spoon

Measuring cup

Airtight container

DIY Step-by-Step:

1. Put 2 cups of the plain lotion into a bowl. Add 8 drops of the chocolate oil and 2 drops of the peanut butter oil, and mix thoroughly. If you want either scent to be stronger, add more oil, 1 drop at a time, until it is as strong as you want it to be.

2. Cut the tips off the vitamin E capsules, and squeeze the oil into the lotion mix. Blend it in thoroughly. (The vitamin E will help make your skin super soft.)

3. Once the ingredients are thoroughly blended, store the Peanut-Butter-Cup Body Frosting in an airtight container. To use, place a small dollop in your hand and rub it into your hands, arms, legs, and feet. Mmmmmmm!

Extra touches: Wash and dry an old lotion bottle, make your own label for it, and use it to store your own Peanut-Butter-Cup Body Frosting concoction. Or, store it in a recycled cake-frosting tub!

Sparkly Vanilla Body Powder

It sparkles! It's vanilla! It's body powder!

Project difficulty: Easy

Materials

1 cup rice flour (available at big supermarkets and for sure at any Asian market or health food store)

⅔ cup cornstarch

Vanilla extract or vanilla essential oil (go to *www.candylandcrafts.com* to find essential oils)

¼ teaspoon fine glitter, any color (available at any craft store—make sure the label specifically states that it is nontoxic)

Tools U Need

Mixing bowl and spoon

Measuring cup

Small scoop (either a small plastic spoon, or a scoop you recycle from a can of coffee or a box of laundry detergent)

Airtight container (an old baby powder bottle, the kind with a shaker on top, works well!)

DIY Step-by-Step:

1. Mix the rice flour and cornstarch in a bowl.
2. Add the glitter and 2 teaspoons of vanilla extract or 8 drops of vanilla oil. Stir all the ingredients, making sure they're blended together very well.
3. Store in an airtight container. To use, sprinkle the powder on your body, or on your bed sheets before you go to sleep!

Extra touch: If you don't have a shaker-type powder bottle available, you could also store the powder in a small butter tub (with a lid) and use a new sponge or a cosmetic puff to apply it.

Banana-Bread Bathballs

These fizzy bathballs are, quite simply, the bomb!

Project difficulty: Moderate

Materials

1 cup baking soda

½ cup cornstarch

½ cup citric acid powder (available at most health food or natural food stores and larger supermarkets)

¾ cup almond or canola oil

Banana essential oil (at *www.candylandcrafts.com*)

Almond essential oil

Yellow food coloring

Tools U Need

Large mixing bowl and spoon

Measuring cup

Wax paper

Ice cream scoop

Plastic wrap

DIY Step-by-Step:

1 Combine the baking soda, cornstarch, and citric acid powder in a bowl.

2 Add the canola or almond oil, 3 or 4 drops of yellow food coloring, and 10 drops each of the banana and almond essential oils. Stir ingredients well, until everything is blended together.

3 Using an ice cream scoop (or a large spoon), form balls of the mixture. Use your hands to shape them into smooth globes. Place them on a sheet of wax paper, and let them dry for 2 days.

4 Wrap each Banana-Bread Bathball individually with plastic wrap. To use, simply drop one in your tub while you're running water for a bath!

Extra touches: Instead of forming the bath bombs into balls, you could also use candy molds to make them into cute little shapes, and use any combination of essential oil flavor you like. You could also use cupcake liners and make Bath Bomb Cupcakes!

Decoupage This! 12 Great Projects for Trying Your Decoupage Talents

Decoupage is a simple, but versatile, craft that essentially involves cutting pieces of paper, gluing them to a surface, then brushing more glue over the surface to seal the paper. You can make some amazing, one-of-a-kind decoupage projects using surfaces like these:

- Shoeboxes
- The top of an old table, or coffee table
- A chair
- A desk
- A dresser for your bedroom
- A stapler, tape dispenser, cup, or empty jar or can that will become your new pencil holder . . . make your whole desk set matching and personalized!
- Photo frames and photo albums
- An old plate that will become a cool serving dish
- Styrofoam balls or old ornaments that will become new ornaments!
- An old telephone
- A blank journal or notebook
- An inexpensive plastic trash can

You've chosen a surface to decoupage . . . but what are you going to use to cover it? Consider these options:

- Wrapping paper, Sunday comics, images from catalogs (Pottery Barn Teen catalog has lots of cool pics), magazines (wedding magazines have great flowers, fabrics, and jewelry images)
- Pages from old paperback novels or photocopies from your favorite children's storybooks
- Old letters, postcards, junk mail, greeting cards
- Food wrappers (clean) from candy, fast food, canned goods
- Photocopies of sheet music, color copies of album or CD covers
- Old calendars, menus, maps, pages from a telephone book, decorative paper napkins
- Your own artwork (or photocopies, so you can frame the originals!), photocopies of your favorite photos

3

My DIY Gifts!

Have you ever received a truly special gift that a friend or family member made *just for you*? If you have, you already know that nothing store-bought can compare to a gift of some-one's time and talent, made especially for you. In this chapter, you'll find dozens of gift ideas—and ideas for dozens more—that will inspire you to get crafting on some fabulous DIY special deliveries of your own!

Fortunate Cookies

What's so fortunate about them? Well, the person who receives a batch of these personalized treats, handmade by you with special messages inside, is definitely one fortunate friend!

Project difficulty: Involved

Materials

2 cups all-purpose flour

8 egg whites (*www.eHow.com* has good instructions on separating egg whites from yolks)

2 cups sugar

9 tablespoons butter (unsalted)

½ teaspoon salt

6 tablespoons heavy whipping cream

½ teaspoon vanilla extract

Cooking spray

Food coloring (whatever color you like)

24 strips of paper, about 2 inches long and ½ inch wide (any type or color of paper will work, as long as you can write on it; you could also print the messages on your computer)

Tools U Need

Wax paper

Large mixing bowl

Measuring cup

Electric mixer

Saucepan

Cookie sheet

Teaspoon

Spatula

Ruler

DIY Step-by-Step:

1. Write messages on all your paper slips, which will be the fortunes for the cookies. Ideas: Use lines of poetry, your favorite knock-knock jokes, inspirational quotes, or personal greetings. Put the paper slips aside.

2. Preheat your oven to 400 degrees, and spray your cookie sheet with cooking spray.

3. Over low heat, melt the butter in a saucepan.

4. In a large bowl, beat the egg whites and sugar with the electric mixer. Once they're combined, add in the flour, salt, butter, vanilla extract, and whipping cream, and continue to beat with the electric mixer until all the ingredients are well combined. Mix in food coloring until the batter is the color you like.

5. Using a teaspoon, drop a spoonful of batter on the greased cookie sheet. Using the back of the spoon, spread the dough out until it forms a thin circle that measures about 2 to 2½ inches across (you can check it with a ruler if you want to be precise). Make 4 or 6 of these on the sheet—leave space between them, because they will spread when baking.

6. Put the cookies in the preheated oven and bake for about 7–8 minutes, checking them to see when the edges turn brown. Once the edges are brown, the cookies are done.

7. Remove the cookies from the oven. Place the cookie sheet on a heat-resistant surface, like a cutting board or the top of the stove (not the countertop!).

8. Working quickly (and carefully!), while the cookies are warm and can still be shaped, slide a spatula under a cookie and place it on a sheet of wax paper.

9. Fold the cookie in half, forming a semicircle with a hollow opening. Pinch it in the middle, on the fold side, and shape it into the shape of a fortune cookie. Again, this must be done quickly, because the cookie will begin to cool right away and be un-bend-y.

10. Once the cookie is shaped, put it on another sheet of wax paper and let it cool. Quickly move on to shape the rest of the cookies before they harden.

11. Once the cookies are cooled, thread your slips of fortune messages through them.

⑫ Repeat until you've used all the batter. The recipe should make about 2 dozen cookies!

Extra touches: Make several different colors of cookies and mix and match them; present the cookies in a Chinese takeout box (available at most craft stores or restaurant supply stores); add a tablespoon or two of cocoa powder to the cookie mix for chocolate Fortunate Cookies; or, on the message slips, write snippets of lyrics from your favorite songs, your favorite movie quotes, or little things that you like about the recipient of this tasty gift!

This Coupon Good for One Week of Free Bedmaking: And Other DIY Coupon Gift Ideas!

Not only are coupon gifts thrifty, they're a DIY present that gives you the opportunity to do something nice for someone else! Check out these ideas

. . . one week of free dogwalking
. . . making book covers for all your best friend's schoolbooks
. . . one batch of cupcakes
. . . a free movie rental, plus snacks
. . . a homemade pizza
. . . one hour of playing a game with your little bro or sister
. . . a free car wash
. . . one week of your best friend raiding your closet
. . . control of the remote control
. . . one week of chores
. . . one free hug! (who wouldn't love to receive this one?)

Chic Chica Evening Wrap

This sparkly shawl will glam up any outfit, whether it's for a party, a dance, or just for school!

Project difficulty: Involved

Materials

4 yards organza fabric, any color, or two shades of the same color, such as pale pink and bubblegum pink or pale green and a brighter, almost lime green (available at a fabric store like Jo-Ann and most craft stores)

6 yards ribbon to match the organza

2½ yards beaded fringe trim or plain fringe trim to match the organza

Needle and thread to match

Tools U Need

Scissors

Tape measure or ruler

An iron

DIY Step-by-Step:

1. Cut two rectangles of fabric, each 36 × 70 inches. If you're using two different colors of fabric, cut one rectangle from each color.

2. With the two "good" sides facing each other (that is, the sides you want facing outward on the finished wrap), sew the two pieces together. Leave half of one short side open.

3. Turn the wrap right side out, and finish sewing the last short side.

4. Cut four pieces of the ribbon, each roughly 36 inches long. Spread the wrap so a short side faces you. Measure up 6 inches from the bottom, and sew one piece of ribbon straight across. Measure down 2 inches from this ribbon (or 4 inches from the bottom) and sew another ribbon straight across. Turn the shawl around so the other short end is facing you, and repeat the process.

5. Now cut two pieces of the beaded fringe or regular fringe trim, each about 36 inches long. Sew a strip to the very edge of each short end.

6. With the iron on the lowest setting, lightly press the two longest seams (those ones without the fringe trim), to make them look neater.

7. Fold the wrap and place it in a pretty, tissue paper-lined box. Tie the box with a piece of the ribbon you used to make the wrap!

Extra touch: If the recipient of the wrap has an upcoming special event, like a prom or a wedding or a formal dance, try to find out what color dress she will be wearing and make the Chic Chica Evening Wrap to match!

Bath-Time Blast Bucket

Anybody on your gift list who still thinks bath-time is a drag will think differently with this simple-to-make pail of DIY goodies!

Project difficulty: Easy

Materials

A plastic pail and shovel, the kind you take to the beach (a great 99-cent store find, and also available at any toy store, home improvement store, or discount retailer)

5–6 sheets craft foam, any thickness, various colors (available at any craft store, in fun pastel and bright colors)

2 cups pure soap flakes (available at craft stores, or in larger supermarkets. You can also make your own flakes by grating a bar of pure soap, like Ivory)

Food coloring, several colors

¼ cup warm water

Tools U Need

Measuring cup

Mixing bowl and spoon

Scissors

Cookie cutters in fun shapes

Ice-cube tray or candy molds

Paint, waterproof stickers, or plastic magnetic letters

Glue gun and glue sticks, or other strong, waterproof glue

DIY Step-by-Step:

1. Spell out the recipient's name with the magnetic letters, and glue them to the bucket. Or paint the name on the bucket.

2. Make bath toys: Cut out various shapes from the craft foam, in different sizes. Trace cookie cutter shapes in pencil, and then cut them out. You can also use stencils, round glasses for circles, or draw freehand shapes like stars, diamonds, horseshoes, hearts, letters, and numbers, and cut them out. These shapes make cool, fun foam toys that will float in the bathtub, and will stick to the tub when wet!

3. Make soap crayon mix: These are washable and safe for "writing" on the tub and the tiles beside the tub. Mix 2 cups of the soap flakes in a bowl with 4 tablespoons of warm water, and stir until it forms a soap paste. This may take quite a bit of stirring, because the paste will be very thick. If you want to make several different colors of soap crayons, divide the soap paste into several smaller bowls and put a drop or two of food coloring into each one.

4. Make soap crayon shapes: Spoon the soap paste into soap molds or into the squares of an ice-cube tray. Press the paste down firmly with a spoon into the cubes or mold shapes. Let them sit in a cool, dry place for at least 48 hours, then pop them out and they're ready to use!

5. Pack the foam shapes and soap crayons into the personalized bucket, along with the shovel. Wrap it in plastic wrap or colorful tissue paper, and tie it with a big ribbon!

Extra touches: Make a batch of Banana-Bread Bathballs or Bubblin' Bath Jam and include them in the Bath-Time Blast Bucket! Other ideas: Include small bouncy balls, a small boat, a brightly colored wash cloth or bath mitt, or some aquatic-themed edible goodies, like gummi fish, Goldfish crackers, or gummi worms.

To You, from Me: Cool Things to Use As Gift Tags!

A gift tag is a great way to make your present, uh, presentation, extra special. Try these simple but cool ideas:

* ❀ Print your own gift labels on the computer.
* ❀ Playing cards—Cover one side by gluing a blank piece of paper to it, and use that side to write your gift message.
* ❀ Flower seed packets—Write your gift message on a sheet of paper, cut it out, and tape it to the back of the seed packet. Tape the packet, with the picture of the flower on top, to your package.
* ❀ A large fake flower—Write your gift message on the flower petals!
* ❀ Holiday ornament—Using a marker, write your gift greeting on an inexpensive holiday ornament ball, and tie the ornament to your package!
* ❀ A miniature chalkboard—Write your gift message on it, then tie, tape, or secure it with a ribbon to the package. It's not only a gift tag, but an extra little gift!
* ❀ Make a paper airplane—Write your message on the airplane wings, and tape it to the gift!
* ❀ A photocopy of a favorite photo—Write a special message on the back, and attach it to the gift. Bonus: Wrap the gift in newspaper, and write the message on a black-and-white photocopied pic for a cool look!
* ❀ A pad of Post-It Notes—Write your message on the first sheet and attach the whole pad to the package. The recipient tears off the message sheet and can use the rest of the notes!
* ❀ A balloon—Blow the balloon up and, temporarily, tie a string around the opening to keep it inflated. Write your message on the balloon, then untie the string and deflate it. Tape or tie it to the package, and tell the recipient to blow it up to read your special note!

Birthday Cake Candle

So easy to make, and so cool to give. Make this your signature birthday gift by making them for all your friends and family members on their special days!

Project difficulty: Moderate

Materials

Foil cupcake liners

1 pound microwavable paraffin wax or several plain white candles you'd like to recycle (paraffin wax is available at most supermarkets or major retailers like Target and Wal-Mart, in the home canning section)

Scented oil (optional, but a fun scent for a Birthday Cake Candle is vanilla or chocolate oil)

Candle wick (available at any craft store; if possible, buy a package of wick assemblies, which is the wick already attached to a wick holder)

2 crayons, the color you want the candle to be

Cake decorating sprinkles, any color and variety

3 store-bought birthday cake candles

Colorful ribbon

Tools U Need

Muffin pan

Microwavable bowl and spoon

Toothpick

DIY Step-by-Step:

1. Stack 4–5 cupcake liners together. You will eventually peel several of them away, but while making the candle, it's best to use several layers for safety. Put the stacks of liners in a muffin pan.

2. Melt the wax in a microwave-safe bowl. Once it's melted, add 2 crayons (with the wrappers removed) and 2 or 3 drops of the

scented oil, if you want to make the candle scented. Return to the microwave for short, 10-second intervals until everything is melted.

3. Drop the wicks into the bottom of the cupcake liners, making sure they come up vertically and past the top of the liner. Fill the cupcake liner with wax up to the top. Let it cool.

4. Test the wax in the cupcake liner with a toothpick. When it is hard enough to hold its shape, spoon some of the wax still in the bowl onto the cupcake. Spread it out so it looks like frosting. You might need to zap the bowl of wax again to make it soft enough to spoon up and spread.

5. Before the wax sets completely, add the cake sprinkles and the three birthday candles to the top of the cupcake.

6. Let the candle set for at least 24 hours.

7. Wrap the candle in plastic wrap, tie it with colorful ribbon, and attach a sweet happy birthday message!

Extra touch: Make several Birthday Cake Candles, package them in a small bakery box (available at most craft stores), and tie them with a ribbon.

Cereal-Box Journal

From the breakfast table to your backpack, there's all kinds of goodness in your favorite cereal. In this DIY gift project, you eat the cereal and then make a journal that's so sweet, you'll want to make an extra one for yourself!

Project difficulty: Easy

Materials

Large cereal box, any kind you like (good idea: find out the favorite cereal of the recipient of the Cereal-Box Journal)

100 sheets three-hole notebook paper (you can substitute a different paper, but you'll have to punch holes in each sheet)

3 individual book rings (available at any office supply or craft store)

Clear contact paper (available at home improvement, hardware, or craft stores) or clear mailing or packing tape

Tools U Need

Scissors and a paper cutter (paper cutter is optional, but will save you time if you have access to one)

A three-hole or single-hole punch

Ruler

DIY Step-by-Step:

1. Carefully, using the seams as a line, cut off the front and back panels of the cereal box. The panel from the front of the box will be the front cover of your journal, and the back panel will be the back cover.

2. Measure the covers. If they are bigger than the paper, cut them down to the same size. If the paper is bigger than the covers, use the paper cutter or scissors to cut the sheets down to the same size as the covers. Just make sure you don't cut off the side of the paper where the holes are!

3. Completely cover both sides of the panels with clear contact paper or with clear packing tape. If using tape, take care to line up the strips evenly and overlap as little as possible.

4. Place a sheet of paper on top of the journal front. Using the punched holes as a guide, mark where the holes should be punched. Punch them. Do the same with the back cover, but have the decorated side of the back of box turned face down when you mark the holes.

5. Line up the front cover, with the sheets of paper underneath it, and the back cover at the bottom of the stack. The three holes should be lined up, down the left side. Insert the book rings, make sure they're securely closed, and your Cereal-Box Journal is ready!

Extra touches: Using the side panels from the cereal box, or a piece cut from an empty milk carton, make a bookmark for the journal; or heat a pin or needle and punch a hole in the handle end of a plastic spoon, thread a piece of ribbon through it and tie it to the top book ring as an extra decoration for the journal. Also, using a single-serving cereal box and paper cut to its size, make a mini notebook to go along with your journal. Other cool journal or notebook cover ideas: macaroni-and-cheese boxes and cookie boxes.

Flowerpot Hairpins

You can buy these adorable hairpin sets in fancy boutiques for $20 and more. But you can DIY the same thing—actually, you can make them even *cuter* yourself—for just a few bucks!

Project difficulty: Easy

Materials

Small terra cotta flowerpot (available at any craft store, usually several for a dollar)

Package of bobby pins (hairpins)

Package of ribbon roses, or any other tiny ribbon flower (available at any craft or fabric store, usually in the ribbon or wedding section)

Package of potting moss (available at any craft store)

1 foot of pretty ribbon

Tools U Need

Glue gun and glue sticks, or other strong glue

Scissors

DIY Step-by-Step:

1 Glue one of the ribbon roses to the flat (top) side of a bobby pin, very near the closed end. Hold it in place several seconds to

make sure it sets. Make at least five more flower pins.

2 Fill the tiny flowerpot with moss all the way to the top.

3 Once the flower pins are dry, push them into the moss, open side first, so the ribbon roses are sticking up out of the moss, like flowers on stems!

4 Tie the ribbon around the top rim of the flowerpot, and you're ready to give this gorgeous gift!

Extra touches: Paint the flowerpot for extra color; spray paint the bobby pins and let them dry thoroughly before you glue the roses to them; or make several Flowerpot Hairpin sets, each with a different color flower, and give them as a "garden" of gifts!

Glamour Gloves

The perfect gift for your favorite gardening buff, these pretty gloves make hands look good even when they're covered in dirt!

Project difficulty: Easy

Materials

1 pair of thick rubber gloves, any color (available at any home improvement or gardening supply store, and some larger drug-stores and discount retailers, and usually available in cool colors like bright yellow and pink)

Toy rings and bracelets (the kind you can find at a party supply store or 99-cent store)

Flat-backed rhinestones, crystals, or beads

Fingernail polish, any color you like

Pretty fabric trim, like pom-poms, lace, fringe, or ribbon, to match the color of the gloves

Tools U Need

Scissors

Glue gun and glue sticks, or other strong glue

Needle and thread

DIY Step-by-Step:

1. Paint the tips of the gloves with the nail polish, to make them look like fingernails.
2. Using a needle and thread or glue, attach the fabric trim you've chosen around the wrist part of each glove.
3. Slip a toy ring or junk jewelry ring over the finger of one glove and glue it into place. Make sure the ring is very loose, so that the recipient's finger can easily slip in and out.
4. Glue inexpensive, sparkly bracelets around each wrist of the gloves and add more rings, if you like, making sure to glue everything into place.
5. Using the rhinestones or beads and glue, decorate the hand part of the gloves.

Extra touch: Wrap the gloves in a box lined with pretty tissue paper, and include a bottle of hand lotion with them. Or carefully fold them and present them inside a small watering can!

Hanging Flower Globe

Who says you can't afford to give someone flowers every day? With this beautiful flower ball, pretty silk flowers will adorn your friend's room at all times. Bonus: These roses have no thorns!

Project difficulty: Easy

Materials

1 8–10-inch Styrofoam ball

50–60 silk flowers with stems, any type and color (Tips: Roses, carnations, and daisies are great for this project. Also, if you're buying the faux flowers at a craft store, you can usually buy them more cheaply if you buy them in bouquets and cut off individual flowers with a short stem on them)

2 feet satiny ribbon (at least 1 inch wide) to match the color of the silk flowers

Tools U Need

Glue gun and glue sticks, or other strong glue

Scissors

DIY Step-by-Step:

1. Put a line of glue all the way around the Styrofoam ball. Press the ribbon into the glue, tie the ends of the ribbon in a knot. Knot the two ends of the ribbon again, so that you have a loop for hanging the Styrofoam ball.
2. Cut the stems off all the fake flowers. Begin gluing the flowers on the ball, until the entire ball is covered.
3. Wrap the Hanging Flower Globe in a box lined with tissue paper, tie a ribbon around the box, and present to your friend!

Extra touches: Instead of using one color of flower, mix and match several, or use two shades of the same color. Also, if you want to make a Hanging Flower Globe for a friend who isn't a big flower fan, you could hot-glue gumdrops, dice, beads, shells, starlight mint candies, M&M's, Skittles, buttons, or small bows to the ball for an equally cool gift!

A Mess O' Marble Magnets

They don't have to match . . . or they can. You don't have to make them all the same size . . . or you can. The only sure thing about these super-cute magnets is that everyone will love them!

Project difficulty: Easy

Materials

Round or flat clear glass marbles in different sizes (available at any craft store)

Pictures, magazine cutouts, interesting paper scraps—any image you want to be the picture in your magnets (more ideas: words cut from magazines, pictures of favorite celebrities, cutouts of cool advertisements, wallpaper or scrapbook paper scraps, photos from food packaging, stickers, comic books, and stamps)

Sheets of magnetic backing (these flexible pieces of magnetic plastic can be cut into shapes—they're available at any craft store)

Tools U Need

Decoupage glue or any glue that dries clear, such as Elmer's

Glue gun and glue sticks, or other strong glue

Small paintbrush or toothpick

Scissors

Pencil

DIY Step-by-Step:

1. Spread the glass marbles out on a flat surface. Place a marble over a picture you want to make into a magnet. Trace around the marble with a pencil, and cut out the picture along the pencil line.

2. Using a paintbrush or toothpick, spread a small amount of the decoupage or Elmer's glue on the back of the marble.

3. Place the marble directly down on top of the picture you have cut out, being careful to smooth out any bubbles in the picture once it's glued to the marble. Once the glue dries, the picture will be crystal clear.

4. Using the glue gun or other strong glue, attach a piece of the magnetic backing to the back of the marble. The piece of magnetic backing should be almost as big as the marble, so that it's strong enough to hold the glass up. Let it set and cement well with the marble.

5. Once the marbles are dry, package them together in a small box.

Extra touches: Package the magnets in a recycled Altoids or other mint tin; or make a themed set of magnets, like a set of Christmas magnets from old holiday cards, a set of Spider Man magnets from an old comic book, or a set of word poetry magnets using letters or words cut from magazines.

The Biocrafty

It's a *biography* that you *craft* for someone special!

Project difficulty: Moderate
(you may want to ask for input from friends and family members of the Biocrafty subject to put together this cool project)

Materials

Blank scrapbook or journal

Photos, mementos, drawings, magazine cutouts, and any other special items that remind you of the person you're making the Biocrafty for

Markers, pens, pencils, stickers, glitter, and other scrapbooking supplies

Various sizes, shapes, colors, and textures of paper

Tools U Need

Scissors

Glue (Elmer's should work fine)

DIY Step-by-Step:

1. Make a list of the things you'd like to include in the Biocrafty. Ideas: Write down your favorite memories of the person, and put one memory on a page, along with a photo, or a drawing or piece of cutout art, that illustrates that memory. Include quotes that remind you of the person. Interview others about the person, and

include their responses. Gather baby photos, old report cards, and other mementos of the past. Make lists of his or her favorite things; make lists of your favorite things about the person. Include photos of your subject's favorite actors, actresses, singers, and so on. Write about his or her hobbies, collections, and other special interests. Write about the person's other friends and family members. Paint or draw a portrait or caricature of your friend. . . . The idea is to make a book that really tells who and what your Biocrafty subject is about, and to let that person know how much you care!

2. Once you have an outline of everything you want to include, decide what order you'd like it to go in. Make a table of contents for the front of the book.

3. Begin writing, gluing, and drawing your content into the book.

4. When you've included all the content you have, go back and embellish the pages. Add rhinestones, beads, page numbers, borders, stickers, and headlines to the pages. Write headlines in glue and cover with glitter. Use bits of ribbon to make frames for pictures. Make polka dots on the pages by dipping a pencil eraser into paint. Use metallic markers to draw gold and silver stars. Use fabric trim to make page or photo borders. Use pieces of old jewelry to decorate the pages. Let your creativity run wild, and you will give your Biocrafty subject a special, personal present that's not only fun to read, but fun to look at, too!

Extra touch: Begin planning a few months ahead of time, and make a Biocrafty for each of your friends and family members for their birthday this year!

4

My DIY Fashion!

How often have you seen a trendy accessory that looked cool but just didn't seem worth the cash? Or maybe you liked the idea of a certain fashion item but thought you could make a better version yourself? Or maybe you have a favorite piece of clothing that you'd like to make over into something new? "My DIY Fashion!" includes ideas for making a skirt out of old ties, fashioning a highly fashionable tote bag out of tape (it's true!), and designing a pair of glamorous beach flip-flops every bit as cool as the fancy ones that sell for $100 but will set you back less than $10! Give your wardrobe a boost, DIY style!

Wraparound Necktie Skirt

Ask all the male members of your family if you can raid their closets for unwanted neckties, or buy a bunch of them at a vintage or
secondhand store, to make this funky skirt that is guaranteed to be
one of a kind wherever you go!

Project difficulty: Involved

Materials

20–25 old neckties, any color, width, style, brand, or style

2 large buttons

Tools U Need

Needle and thread—if you know how to use a sewing machine or
know someone who can help you use one, your project will be much
easier and will take less time!

Tape measure or ruler

Scissors

Piece of chalk

DIY Step-by-Step:

1. Spread all the ties out side by side on a flat surface, with each
   one lying flat. The ties should all be oriented the same way, tops
   and bottoms together.
2. Arrange them in the order you want them to be in your finished
   skirt. Place the ties side by side, so that they touch. The wid-
   est part of the ties will go at the bottom of the skirt, which will
   make it flare out in an A-line shape.
3. With the tape measure, measure your waist to determine how
   big the skirt will need to be. Add 3 inches to that number. Measure the width of the row of ties at the top, where it is narrowest,
   and make sure it equals your waist measurement plus 3 inches.
   The 3 inches gives you extra skirt for the wraparound—if you

want extra wraparound, you can add more inches.

4. Sew the ties together, at the sides, from the top all the way to the bottom. Once you've sewn them all, do a quick test to make sure the skirt will be wide enough to wrap around your waist, with a few extra inches for the wraparound. If it's not wide enough, just sew a few more ties to the tie fabric until it fits!

5. Once you're sure the fabric is the right width, it's time to decide on the length of the skirt. Hold the tie fabric against your waist so that the wide, pointed part is at the bottom. Move the fabric up and down to decide how long you want the skirt to be. When you've found the proper length, use the chalk to mark where the skirt's waistline should be. This is where you will need to cut the tie fabric so that the skirt will be the desired length. Don't cut yet, though! Once you've marked the spot, cut 3 inches above that spot, so that you'll have enough material to make a hem at the top.

6. Fold the top 1½ inches down to the inside of the fabric, so that the fold doesn't show from the outside. The bottom of the fold will lie along the line you marked for your waistline. Sew the waistline down along that line.

7. Sew one large button at the top edge of the skirt (if the ties are laying flat, with the design side up, that would mean you would be sewing a button on the top left corner).

8. With chalk in hand, pick up the skirt, which should now be the correct length, and wrap it around your waist (it might be helpful to have another person helping you for this part), folding the left side of the skirt toward you first, and then having the right side of the skirt overlap. Adjust the overlap so that it is comfortable, and look in a mirror to make sure the skirt hangs the way you want it to.

9. Using the chalk, mark the spot where the left edge of the skirt meets the right side. Sew a button onto the spot. This button will be on the outside of the left edge, so it will button into the waistline.

10. Also, with the chalk, mark the spot where the outside edge of the skirt meets the fabric behind it. Sew a button onto that spot, onto the fabric behind the skirt's front edge.

11. With the skirt wrapped around you, again mark on the fabric where the buttons line up with the fabric in front of them. In those two spots, cut buttonholes (holes should be the width of the button, plus ¼ inch). Once you've cut the holes, sew simple stitches around them to keep them from fraying, and test them to make sure they're big enough to get the button through, but not so big that the button will slip out.

12. Whew! After a lot of hard work and patience, your groovy new skirt should be ready to make its debut!

Extra touches: If you want a skirt that's a specific color, try to use ties that are only that color; you could also try to use the same pattern of ties, like all striped ties, all paisley ties, all polka dot ties, and so on; since many older ties are lined, you may want to consider opening the seams and removing the lining from them before you use them in the skirt, because they can make the end result very heavy; for a great top to go with your Wraparound Necktie Skirt, take a plain T-shirt and sew an old tie to the front of it!

Barbie Clothes Tote Bag (with Matching Barbie Shoe Earrings!)

Even if you're not into Barbie anymore, you have to admit—that chica has the coolest wardrobe around! This project takes a plain, inexpensive tote bag and one of your favorite old Barbie outfits and turns them into a designer-like bag that even Barbie would be proud to carry around! And oh, how you will love the matching earrings!

Project difficulty: Easy

Materials

Plain tote bag, any size and color you want (available at any craft store, or you could recycle an old one you already have)

Complete Barbie outfit, including shoes and accessories (at thrift stores, 99-cent stores, and toy stores)

Extra pair of Barbie shoes or boots

Fabric paint or markers, or flat-backed beads, rhinestones, or crystals

Earring backings (also called findings, available at any craft store or bead store)

Tools U Need

Scissors

Glue gun and glue sticks, or other strong glue

DIY Step-by-Step:

1. Arrange the Barbie outfit on the tote bag, in any way that you think it looks good. Glue it into place.
2. Add some detail to the bag with beads, crystals, or rhinestones. Use them to spell out your name, or a phrase like "Glamour Girl" or "Rock Star." Or paint stars around the outfit with the fabric paint. And now your tote is, well, in the bag!
3. For the matching Barbie earrings: Glue each extra Barbie shoe to an earring backing. If the earring backings require a hole in the shoe, punch a small hole through the plastic with a needle or safety pin, and stick the backing through the shoes. And you have matching Barbie Clothes Tote Bag and Barbie Shoe Earrings. Now if only we could figure out a way to make that Barbie Dream House life-sized . . .

Extra touch: If your tote bag is big enough, and you're willing to sacrifice a Barbie (or you can find a used one at a thrift store or yard sale), you could put the outfit on Barbie and use really strong glue to attach Barbie herself to your tote!

Duct-Tape Bag

Don't believe you can make a cool tote bag with nothing more than some tape and cardboard? It's true! In fact, this DIY bag is so cool that all your friends will be asking you to make Duct-Tape Bags for them!

Project difficulty: Moderate

Materials

Duct tape, in any color you want

Piece of cardboard, 10 inches wide and 5 inches long

Tools U Need

Scissors

DIY Step-by-Step:

1. Begin building the sides of your bag. One by one, cut six pieces of duct tape, each about 10 inches long. Spread the first piece on a flat surface, horizontally, with the sticky side up. Spread the next piece just below it, so that the top barely overlaps (and sticks to) the bottom of the first strip.

2. Cut and attach four more pieces of tape in the same way. At the end, you will have a sheet of tape, 10 inches wide and 8 inches (six strips) long, sticky side up.

3. One by one, cut six more pieces of tape. As you cut each one, carefully stick it to your sheet of tape (sticky sides together) so that the strips line up. You will end up with one big, double-sided sheet of tape.

4. Repeat steps 1 through 3 two more times, so that in the end you have three double-sided sheets of tape of the exact same size. You can use any color you want, or mix and match for a funkier look!

5. From one of the sheets, cut two strips, 4 inches by 10 inches each; these will become the sides of your bag.

6. Completely cover the strip of cardboard with tape; this will be the bottom of your bag.

7. Begin attaching the pieces to shape the bag. Attach the front and back panel to the bottom panel, taping them together both inside and outside. Now attach the two sides to the rest of the bag, again taping both inside and out.

(8) Make handles—make them as long as you want them to be—by taping two pieces of tape together (sticky sides facing each other) and taping them to the top of the bag.

(9) You've got a stylin' Duct-Tape Bag!

Extra touches: And now comes the really fun part: decorating the bag! Some ideas: Use different colors of tape to make the bag striped. Using various colors of tape, cut out little flowers or polka dots and place them all over the bag. Use one color of tape for the bag and another color for the handles. Cover a smaller piece of cardboard with tape and tape it to the inside or outside of the bag (or both!) to make pockets.

That's Just Duct-y: 3 Other Cool Projects You Can Make from Duct Tape

Duct tape . . . it's not just for fixing leaky pipes anymore. In fact, duct tape now comes in so many different colors—everything from pink and purple to camouflage and fluorescent green—that it's as famous for its DIY crafting possibilities as it is for its DIY home-repair uses! Available at most home improvement, craft, and discount retailer stores, duct tape is a groovy way to make a fashion statement that's sure to stick!

    Duct tape wallet: Go to *www.ducktapeclub.com* and click the "Duck-Tivities" link.

    Duct tape ribbon and bow: To decorate a package with duct tape ribbon and bow, wrap one strip of tape all the way around the package, horizontally. Wrap another strip all the way around the package, vertically. For the bow, take one long strip of tape (8 to 10 inches) and fold one end over the other, forming a loop. Press the loop together, making the sticky sides touch in the middle (you should have something that looks like a figure eight). Cut seven or eight more strips, the same size as the first, and attach them to the first loop in the same way, making several figure-eight shapes that overlap in the middle, forming a duct-y bow!

    Duct tape rose: Go to *www.ducktapeclub.com* and click the "Duck-Tivities" link.

Duct-Tape Folder

What better accessory for your Duct-Tape Bag than a Duct-Tape Folder?

Project difficulty: Moderate

Materials

Duct tape, in any color you want

Tools U Need

Scissors

Ruler

DIY Step-by-Step:

1. Cut one strip of tape, 18 inches long. Spread it on a flat surface, sticky side up.
2. Cut six more strips of the same length. One by one, attach the strips to each other: Spread each next strip just below the previous one, so that its top edge overlaps and sticks to the bottom of the previous one. When you've attached all of the pieces, you will have a large rectangle of tape, sticky side up.
3. One by one, cut seven more pieces of tape, each 18 inches long. Carefully stick each piece of tape to the rectangle you've already made, sticky sides together, so that the strips line up. At the end, you'll have one big, double-sided sheet of tape, which should roughly measure 18 inches wide by seven strips (12 inches) long.
4. Now make two smaller sheets, using the same method. The smaller sheets should measure 8½ inches wide, and about three or four strips (5 or 6 inches) long.
5. Fold the large sheet in half, making a folder.
6. Now make pockets on the inside of the folder. Tape one of the smaller sheets to each of the inner sides. Tape each small sheet to the folder on three sides, and leave the top open.

7. Now, again, the fun part: Decorate the folder with tape cutouts or polka dots; make stripes with other colors of tape; or personalize your folder by spelling out your name with tape on the front!

Flowery Flip-Flops

Perfect for the beach, but so cute you'll be wearing them with skirts and dresses all summer!

Project difficulty: Easy

Materials

1 pair plain rubber flip-flops, your size, any color (flips-flops are a great 99-cent store and discount drugstore find)

2 large plastic flowers (available at any craft store or garden supply center)

Rhinestones, crystals, or beads

Tools U Need

Glue gun and glue stick, or other strong glue (whatever glue you use should be waterproof)

Scissors

DIY Step-by-Step:

1. Cut any stems off the plastic flowers so that the flowers have flat backs.

2. Glue the flowers to the top of each flip-flop, making sure they won't rub against your toes when you put the sandals on.

3. Decorate with the rhinestones, crystals, or beads. Some ideas: Glue some of the beads to the middle of the flowers for extra detail; glue beads along the outsides of the flip-flops (but don't decorate the tops, where your feet go); or glue beads along the straps of the flip-flops.

④ Let the shoes dry for at least a few hours before you wear them.

Extra touch: Flowery Flip-Flops make great gifts for friends headed off to live in a college dorm or for a stay at summer camp.

Paper-Bead Necklace

Can't find beads you like, or don't want to pay several dollars *per bead*? No prob. Just find some interesting paper and a little glue and make your own!

Project difficulty: Easy

Materials

Pretty scrapbook paper, magazine pages, wrapping paper, or any other paper that has interesting and colorful patterns

Strong glue that dries clear

Beading twine or thread (or strong fishing line or waxed dental floss)

Random plain round beads

Tools U Need

Paintbrush

Knitting needle or chopstick

Scissors

Ruler

Pencil

DIY Step-by-Step:

① Using a ruler, measure out and draw a bunch of triangles on your chosen paper. Make the bottom of the triangle as wide as you want your bead to be. If your triangle is 2 inches wide at the bottom, your bead will be 2 inches long. No matter how wide they are at the bottom, your triangles should measure about 10 inches from bottom to top. Cut the triangles out of the paper.

2. Turn the triangles so that the pattern you want to see on the bead is face down. Begin at the wide, bottom end of the triangle and start wrapping the paper around the chopstick or knitting needle.

3. Continue wrapping the strip of paper until you get to the top (the pointy end). Once you have just a bit of paper left, brush some glue on the tip of the paper and seal it to the rest of the roll. Then brush a bit of the glue on the outside of the rolled tri-angle to strengthen the seal . . . you've just made a bead! Leave the bead on the chopstick or knitting needle for a few minutes, so that it can dry.

4. Make several more beads, either with the same paper or by mixing and matching.

5. String the beads on the beading string, threading a paper bead, then a plain round bead, then a paper bead, and so on, until you have a full necklace. Tie it off, or purchase a necklace clasp, and you're ready to show off your handiwork!

Extra touches: You could paint the paper beads; dip them in glue and sprinkle them with glitter; make one really large bead (by mea-suring out a wider-bottomed triangle) and use it at the center of your necklace; and make a bracelet to match your necklace.

Plush Polar Poncho

Polar bears make you think of the cold, right? But you'll feel noth-ing but warm and fuzzy with this fuzzy polar-fleece poncho that is so simple to make!

Project difficulty: Moderate

Materials

60-inch by 60-inch piece of white polar fleece

Fabric trim (pom-poms, fringe trim, and beaded trim all look great on this project!)

Embroidery thread and needle (optional)

Beads, crystals, or rhinestones (optional)

Tools U Need

Waterproof fabric glue

Measuring tape or ruler

Scissors

Pencil

DIY Step-by-Step:

1. Spread the polar fleece on a flat surface. Measure it to make sure it is a perfect square. (It's okay if it isn't exactly 60 inches on each side, but all the sides should be the same width and length.)

2. Fold the square into a triangle, with the fold at the top. Fold the fabric in half on the diagonal (bring a top corner down over the opposite bottom corner), so that the square becomes a triangle. Turn the triangle so that the fold is at the top of the triangle and the bottom corner is nearest you.

3. Using the ruler, measure the point at the center of the fold. Mark this point with a pencil.

4. From the center point, measure 8 inches to the right and to the left. Mark these points with a pencil.

5. From each of these three points, measure 5 inches straight down. Mark these points with a pencil.

6. Use a ruler to draw lines connecting the points you've made into a rectangle 16 inches long and 5 inches deep. The fold will be the top line of this rectangle. Keep the fleece folded, and cut out the rectangle, cutting through both layers of the fleece. That's the neck hole, and now you have a poncho!

7. The white fleece is so pretty that you may want to leave it just as it is. But if you'd like to spruce it up, you can decorate it any way you want. Glue beads or crystals randomly all over it; glue

fringe trim all along the edges or along the neck hole; or use embroidery thread and needle to make small designs along the edges or along the neck hole.

Extra touches: You could use any color of fleece you like; make tassels or large pom-poms to hang from the edges of the poncho; or you could use iron-on or sew-on appliqués to spruce up the poncho.

Polka-Dot Tee

This fun T-shirt will look great with a pair of jeans, or under a cardigan sweater that matches the color of the polka dots!

Project difficulty: Easy

Materials

A T-shirt in your size (any color will work, but a white one makes the polka dots really pop!)

3 bottles fabric paint, each a different color (pick any color combo you like—some ideas include three shades of the same color; red, blue, and yellow; and yellow, green, and blue)

Tools U Need

Circle stencils in at least three different sizes (available at any craft store; you can also make your own circle stencils by tracing different-sized drinking glasses onto stiff cardboard and cutting the circle shape out)

Paintbrush

Large piece of thick cardboard or a magazine you no longer want

DIY Step-by-Step:

1. Make sure your T-shirt is washed and ironed.
2. Spread the T-shirt on a flat surface, the front side facing up.

Between the front and back layer of the shirt, place a piece of heavy cardboard or a magazine.

3 Position a stencil somewhere on the shirt. Hold it in place, or temporarily tape it into place for extra support, and begin painting inside the stencil with the fabric paint.

4 Once you're done with the first circle, carefully pick up the stencil—you don't want to smudge your perfect circle—and move it to another place on the shirt. Paint another circle in a different color. Continue this process, using different colors and different circle sizes, until you have as many circles as you like on the shirt.

5 Let the shirt dry for several hours, and it will be ready to wear!

6 Important tips: Make sure the cardboard or magazine backing is between the front and back of the shirt at all times. If it isn't, the paint might seep through to the back of the shirt. Also, if you are using one paintbrush for the whole project, make sure you have a container of warm water to wash out the brush before you switch to a new paint color.

Retro Cool Tank Top

An inexpensive tank top—available for under $10 at any discount retailer—becomes a dressy summer shirt with a simple piece of fabric trim, a single fake flower, and a smidgen of glitter!

Project difficulty: Easy

Materials

Plain black tank top, in your size

1 single stem silk flower, light or bright pink

5 feet of pretty ribbon or fabric trim in a similar shade of pink

Glitter

Tools U Need

Blank pin back (available at any craft or fabric store)

Needle and thread

Glue gun and glue sticks

Paintbrush, cotton swab, or toothpick

Scissors

DIY Step-by-Step:

1. Cut the stem off the flower so that the back of the flower is flat. Dip the paintbrush, cotton swab, or toothpick into the glue and lightly "paint" the petals of the flower with it. While the glue is still wet, hold the flower over a piece of paper, and sprinkle a generous amount of the glitter over the places where you painted on glue. Shake the excess glitter off the flower and onto the paper—you can put the excess glitter back into its bottle. Let the flower dry for a few minutes. Then glue the pin back to the back of the flower, and put it aside to dry.

2. Cut a piece of ribbon or fabric trim that is long enough to go all the way around the bottom edge of your tank top. Sew it into place. You could also use fabric glue to secure it into place, but sewing it ensures it will stay attached when you wash it.

3. Before you wear the tank top, pin the glittery flower to one of the shoulders. Sleek black top, pretty pink trim, and beautiful pink flower . . . you've got one Retro Cool Tank Top!

4. Before you wash the top, make sure you remove the flower pin, and wash the top in a gentle cycle.

Extra touch: If black and pink isn't your thing, try other color combinations. Some ideas: brown tank with pink trim and pink flower, white tank with peach trim and peach flower, pale blue tank with red trim and a red flower, or black tank with red trim and a red flower (very dressy!).

Ribbon Belt

This nifty accessory can set you back $20 or more in fancy boutiques and retail clothing stores. But for about 15 minutes of your time, you can make a DIY version for just a few bucks!

Project difficulty: Easy

Materials

Plain fabric web belt (the kind baseball players wear with their uniforms), any color you like (you can find these at any sporting goods store or a sports uniform supply store)

Piece of ribbon 5 feet long, and roughly 1 inch wide, in a color that will go well with the color of the web belt (most web belts are about 1¼ inches wide, so you can use any width of ribbon as long as it is at least ½ inch less wide than the belt)

Tools U Need

Fabric glue

Scissors

DIY Step-by-Step:

1. Spread the belt out on a flat surface.
2. Cut a length of ribbon as long as the belt, minus the belt buckle.
3. Using a generous amount of the fabric glue, cover the back of the piece of ribbon. Starting at one end, glue the ribbon so it runs right down the middle of the belt.
4. Press the ribbon onto the belt, smoothing out any bubbles. Leave the belt flat to dry for at least an hour, and then buckle up!

Extra touch: Web belts are so inexpensive—usually under $5 each—that you could make several, for yourself and to give as gifts to friends!

From Dull to Designer: 7 Quick Ways to Take a Plain T-Shirt from Frumpy to Fabulous!

Most craft stores sell plain T-shirts, in many colors, for as little as $2 or $3 each, and you can find plain white tees—look in the men's or boy's sections—at most discount retailers and department stores in packages of four or five that cost around $1 each! So grab a few T-shirts, and make a new fashion statement with these cool ideas!

- ✿ Sew or use fabric glue to attach a pretty grosgrain ribbon around the sleeves of the shirt. Make or buy ribbon roses, and sew or use fabric glue to put them all around the neck and bottom hem of a fitted tee.
- ✿ Cut off the sleeves from two different-colored T-shirts. Sew the sleeves back on . . . the "wrong" shirt!
- ✿ On your computer, type a favorite quote (from a favorite song, movie, or TV show) in a great font. Print it out on iron-on transfer paper and iron it onto a colored tee. Also find the perfect quote on the Web at *www.quotationspage.com*; *www.brainyquote.com*; or *www.quoteland.com*.
- ✿ Use fabric glue to make a random pattern, or to spell your name, with rhinestones or crystals on the front of the T-shirt.
- ✿ Make a collage of your favorite photos of your friends. Scan the collage into your computer and print it out on iron-on transfer paper. Iron it onto your shirt.
- ✿ Embroider flowers of different colors on the front of your shirt. Other ideas: Embroider your initials on the front, simple shapes or different-colored lines around each sleeve, or tiny flowers all around the neck.
- ✿ Around the sleeves and neck of a short-sleeved T-shirt, glue or sew inexpensive lace trim, available in many colors at any large craft store. The simple but elegant result will look good with jeans or a skirt!

Sweet Treats Cosmetic Bag

If you're a fan of the Duct-Tape Bag, this cute little cosmetic goody bag will be the perfect accessory for holding your lip gloss, nail polish, tissues, change, gum, and other small items that always seem to fall to the bottom of your bag! P.S.: All the supplies you need for this project can usually be found at 99-cent stores!

Project difficulty: Moderate

Materials

24 (at least) square candy wrappers, like those from Starburst, Blow Pops, Dum Dum lollipops, or Tootsie Roll Pops—if you use Starburst, you may need more, since they're smaller

Old shower curtain or shower curtain liner

Tools U Need

Industrial-strength Velcro tape

Clear mailing tape

Scissors

Measuring tape or ruler

DIY Step-by-Step:

1. Spread all the candy wrappers flat, and smooth them out as much as possible. Cut a rectangular piece of the shower curtain or liner that measures 15 inches wide by 6 inches long. Set it aside.

2. Cut a 15-inch strip of clear mailing tape. Spread it, horizontally, on a flat surface with the sticky side up. Cut another strip of the tape the same length. Place this strip beneath the first one, with the top of the new piece barely overlapping and sticking to the bottom of the first one. Continue cutting and overlapping them until you have a large rectangle of tape, sticky side up, that measures 15 inches wide and 6 inches long. (Cut away any excess beyond those measurements.)

3. Begin sticking the wrappers to the sheet of tape, one next to each other, so they form a row. Continue sticking down rows of wrappers until the entire rectangle of tape is covered. If the wrappers hang over the tape, cut off the excess wrappers.

4. Cut a 15-inch long strip of tape, and put it very carefully straight across the top of the rectangle, so it lines up with the strip of tape on the bottom (under the candy wrappers). Continue covering the candy wrappers with clear tape, one strip at a time, being careful to keep the strips of tape straight and to just barely overlap them.

5. Repeat steps 1 and 2, to create another sticky rectangle measuring 15 × 6 inches. Cut a same-sized piece of shower curtain or liner. Press the shower curtain on top of the tape, with the good side (the side you will want to show as the inside of the cosmetic bag) face down on the tape. Be careful to keep the shower curtain flat—no wrinkles!

6. Place the sheet of wrappers on top of the shower curtain, with the wrappers face up. Line up the edges of the shower curtain and the candy wrappers—these two layers are about to become one! Cut more strips of tape, with neat edges, this time 16 inches long. One by one, cover the candy wrappers with these strips, being careful to keep each one straight and barely overlapped with the previous strip. Position the strips evenly so that you have an extra ½ inch at each side. Fold and stick those ends under.

7. You should now have one single sheet, 6 inches wide by 15 inches long, with the candy wrappers showing on one side and the shower curtain or liner on the other. Turn the sheet over, so the candy wrapper side is face up, and the sheet is sitting with a short end nearest you.

8. Measure up 5 inches from the bottom, and place the ruler across the sheet. Pick up the bottom of the sheet and fold along that line. Crease the fold by running your finger back and forth over it several times.

9. Cut a strip of tape 5 inches long, and tape one folded side together. Cut another strip, and tape the other folded side. Leave the top open, so that you now have a pocket!

10 Turn the pocket inside out, which will put the right side (candy
    wrappers) out. Spread the sheet flat, with the pocket face up. At
    the bottom of the pocket, in the middle, stick the sticky side of
    the Velcro tape.

11 Fold down the top of the sheet so that it meets the bottom of the
    pocket. You have now formed your cosmetic bag, which should
    measure 6 inches wide and 5 inches tall! Mark the spot on the
    top of the sheet where it touches the Velcro. Attach the other
    part of the Velcro there. Your Sweet Treats Cosmetic Bag is now
    complete and ready to be loaded up with your beauty goodies!

Extra touch: If you want a little change pocket inside the cosmetic
bag, place a wrapper, face side up, against the back of the bag on
the inside, and tape it on three sides.

5

My DIY Party!

You don't need expensive food and decorations to throw a party—all you do need is tasty food, fun decorations, good friends, and a little creativity. A fun theme doesn't hurt either, and this chapter should give you plenty of ideas for gathering your favorite people together for a celebration!

Party Planner: Nine Reasons to Throw a Party
(As If You Ever *Need* an Excuse to Throw a Party!)

Yep, any time is a good time for a party, and it will be all the more fun if you have a theme!

A Super Sundae Party

Invite your friends over for a sundae bar party! Send out invitations in the shape of an ice cream cone. Have everyone make their own Coffee-Can Ice Cream (recipe in this chapter), and set up a table with dishes full of sundae toppings, like chopped-up candy bars, ice cream cones and crushed ice cream cones, fresh berries (strawberries, raspberries, and blueberries are always favorites), cake sprinkles, chocolate chips, coconut, crushed graham crackers, strawberry jam, crushed cookies, chocolate syrup, caramel, granola, cereal (Cap'n Crunch is amazing on vanilla ice cream!), walnuts, peanuts, marshmallow crème, and mini marshmallows. You could also have a similar type of party with a pizza bar, taco bar, or waffle bar!

A Candy Land Party

It's all about candy with this sweet (pardon the pun) soiree! Send out invitations written on a piece of paper and wrapped around a Hershey bar, play that old favorite board game, Candy Land, make Yummy Gummies (recipe in this chapter), and decorate with Candy-Tree Centerpieces (instructions in this chapter)!

A Tea Party

Send invitations shaped like teacups or tea bags, make Cookie-Cutter Finger Sandwiches (recipe in this chapter), make Flowerpot Hairpins (from Chapter 3) for all your guests, and, of course, make all kinds of hot tea (Celestial Seasonings makes tea in every flavor you can imagine) and iced tea (add in yummy slices of fresh fruit like lemon, lime, orange, and strawberry, or sprigs of fresh mint)!

A Christmas in July Party

It's the middle of summer, and you want a theme to get friends together, give them gifts, and eat some yummy food? Christmas in

(continued)

July is your theme! Send out invitations in the shape of a Christmas tree or Santa (or use leftover holiday cards from last year), make Photo Cube Bookends (from Chapter 1) with personalized photos of everyone for all your pals, and serve up Edible Balloon Bowls (recipe in this chapter) full of red and green M&M's!

A Winter Day-at-the-Beach Party

If you can have Christmas in July, then why not have a beach party in December or January? Buy cheapo beach balls at a 99-cent store, blow them up, write the invitation information on them, deflate them, and send them to guests! Serve Goldfish crackers, fish sticks, and fruit juices with little paper umbrellas. Make a centerpiece with a big fish bowl filled with blue Jell-O, Nerds for gravel on the bottom of the bowl, and gummi fish "swimming" in the Jell-O, and have a table full of supplies for friends to make their own Flowery Flip-Flops (from Chapter 4)!

A Film-Festival Party

Write the invitation on a piece of paper and wrap it around a bag of microwavable popcorn, set up a candy stand on a small table (buy boxes of movie candy at a discount or 99-cent store), make lots of popcorn with different flavors (see the Popcorn Pop-Ins sidebar, in this chapter), have plenty of ice-cold sodas on hand, and load up the DVD player or VCR with great flicks! Suggestions: *Freaky Friday*, *A Cinderella Story*, *Confessions of a Teenage Drama Queen*, *Say Anything*, *Pretty in Pink*, *Big*, *Toy Story*, *Shrek*, *Good Will Hunting*, *Bruce Almighty*, *My Girl*, *Edward Scissorhands*, *Selena*, *Clueless*, and *Legally Blonde*!

A Spa Party

It's a day of pampering for you and your best buds! For invitations, write the party info on a slip of paper, roll it up, and tie it with a ribbon to a small bottle of nail polish (you can get nice colors on sale at a 99-cent store or a discount drugstore). Select several beauty projects from Chapter 2 to make with your guests, serve healthy and tasty food like fruit kebobs (see the March 16 DIY-a-Day calendar entry for recipe), Cookie-Cutter Finger Sandwiches

(continued)

(this chapter), and ice water with fruit slices, and decorate the party with sparkling Le Chandelier de Plastic Cups (from Chapter 1)!

A Trash-to-Treasure Party

Get rid of stuff you don't want, and snag some new (well, new to you) stuff! Send invitations to friends on—what else?—junk mail (write the party info on the back of the envelope). Ask them to bring stuff they no longer want—books, CDs, DVDs, clothes, shoes, jewelry, hats, scarves, magazines, craft goodies, toys, bags, stuffed animals, anything someone else might want—to the party. Once everyone arrives, have them put their unwanted goodies (plus stuff you want to trade) in a big circle in the middle of the floor. Everyone stands in a circle. Go around the circle, with each person allowed to pick one item from the pile (pick numbers from a hat to see who goes first). Once everyone has gone twice, have them stash their newfound treasures in another room. Now the really fun part: Everyone puts price tags on the remaining goodies, sets them up on tables in your front yard or garage, and waits for the customers to come to your very own yard sale! You can all split the profits, or agree to donate them all to a great charity! Preparty preparations: Find out if there are local newspapers that let you run free yard-sale notices, and put up signs around your neighborhood, at school (only if it's okay with your principal, of course), and at the super-market. Make sure you have plenty of cold drinks on hand (fill a large bucket with ice and load it up with cans of soda and juice); and prepare some yummy snacks, like Candy-and-Fruit Pizza (see recipe in this chapter)!

And, Of Course, a DIY Party!

Invite your friends over to find out just how fun it is to be a crafty girl! Send out invitations written on a recipe card (use colored index cards and write the party details in a recipe format), pick one or two projects from this book for everyone to make, ask each guest to bring one of the materials needed in the projects (you supply the rest), and prepare plenty of fun food for your busy day of DIY-ing, like Yummy Gummies (recipe in this chapter)!

Yummy Gummies

Gummies are not just for bears anymore! With this simple recipe, you can make gummi candies into any shape you want, using chocolate candy molds. Perfect for a Candy Land party, no?

Project difficulty: Easy

Materials

6 boxes unflavored gelatin

2 boxes Jell-O, any flavor you want

2 envelopes Kool-Aid, any flavor you want

1 cup cold water

Tools U Need

Candy molds (available at any craft or baking supply store)

Microwave-safe mixing bowl and spoon

Airtight container

DIY Step-by-Step:

1. Mix the gelatin, Jell-O, Kool-Aid, and water together in a bowl. Stir well and make sure everything is mixed together very well. The mixture should start to become very thick.
2. Put the bowl in the microwave and cook for 1 minute. Check the mix. It should start to become foamy on top. If it isn't, continue to cook it in the microwave for 10-second intervals, checking it every 10 seconds to see if it has started to get foamy on top.
3. Once the mix is ready, use a spoon to carefully fill your candy molds (you could also use a turkey baster to fill the molds).
4. Put the molds into the freezer for 10–15 minutes. Once they have set, remove the trays from the freezer and pop out the gummies (a toothpick may help loosen them from the mold). Store them in an airtight container, and enjoy!

Candy-and-Fruit Pizza

There's pizza, then there's dessert pizza! Almost as much fun to make as it is to eat—well, *almost*—your friends will be surprised by how much it looks like a regular pizza and tastes like all your favorite desserts rolled into one!

Project difficulty: Easy

Materials

1 roll refrigerated sugar-cookie dough

1 can vanilla cake frosting

Red food coloring

Grapes, kiwi fruit, strawberries, and bananas

M&M's

Shredded coconut

Chocolate syrup (or make your own by melting chocolate chips in the microwave)

Tools U Need

Pizza baking pan

Butter knife (for spreading frosting)

Spoon

DIY Step-by-Step:

1. Preheat your oven according to the directions on the cookie dough package. Open the cookie dough and spread it onto the pizza pan, covering the whole pan. Bake the dough, according to the package directions. Remove the pan from the oven and let the dough cool for at least an hour.

2. Open the tub of cake frosting and mix in several drops of red food coloring. Stir it in well until the frosting is the color you want it to be.

3. Make sure the cookie has cooled completely, and spread the frosting over the entire cookie.

4. Now, the fun part: Decorate your pizza with the candy and fruit toppings! Ideas: Use red M&M's to look like pepperonis, coconut to look like shredded cheese, banana slices to look like peppers, strawberries to look like tomatoes, and sliced grapes and kiwi fruit to look like olives and mushrooms.

5. Sprinkle another layer of coconut across the pizza. Put melted chocolate or chocolate syrup into a plastic sandwich baggie, snip off a tiny corner, and drizzle it across the pizza! Yum!

Extra touch: Ask a manager at your favorite local pizzeria for a few empty (unused!) pizza boxes the next time you order, and serve your Candy-and-Fruit Pizzas in them!

Popcorn Pop-Ins: A Few Quick Ways to Spice Up Your Corny Snacks

Mix melted butter and one of these tasty flavorings:

* ❀ Chili powder
* ❀ Garlic powder
* ❀ Cinnamon
* ❀ Onion powder
* ❀ Cocoa powder
* ❀ Barbeque seasoning powder
* ❀ Grated Parmesan cheese
* ❀ Taco seasonings

Candy-Tree Centerpieces

Money may not grow on trees (don't your parents always tell you that?), but candy does—at least on these cool party centerpieces! Bonus: The candy on the tree remains edible, and you can even make smaller versions of the candy trees and use them as take-home favors for your party guests!

Project difficulty: Moderate

Materials

1 large Styrofoam cone and 1 small Styrofoam ball, any size, though remember that the size will determine how big your final tree will be, i.e., for a centerpiece, use larger Styrofoam pieces, for mini favors, use smaller ones (available at any craft store)

1 wooden dowel, about twice as long as the Styrofoam cone (available at any craft store)

1 large terra cotta flower pot (just big enough to fit the Styrofoam ball)

1–2 pounds of wrapped candy, like fun-size candy bars, M&Ms, and Tootsie Rolls

Ribbon

Tools U Need

Glue gun and glue sticks, or other super strong glue (like e6000, available at any craft or hardware store)

DIY Step-by-Step:

1. Push the dowel into the Styrofoam cone, so that the flat part is on the bottom. Secure it with the glue. Insert the other end of the dowel into the Styrofoam ball—several inches of the dowel should remain visible—and secure it with glue.

2. Cover the Styrofoam ball with glue, and push it into the terra cotta pot so that the bottom is in firm contact with the bottom of the pot. Center the ball so that the dowel and the Styrofoam cone stick straight up. Hold the dowel up until the glue starts to set and the Styrofoam ball stays in place. Let the glue dry for at least 30 minutes.

3. Now, begin building your candy tree! Starting at the bottom of the Styrofoam cone, use a small dab of glue on the edge of a candy wrapper and stick it to the cone. Hold it in place for a

few seconds until it sets. Continue gluing the candy all the way around the bottom edge until you have a whole row of candy.

④ Start another row on top of the bottom one, and continue gluing the candy around the Styrofoam cone until the entire cone is covered, and no Styrofoam is visible. Smaller candies like Tootsie Rolls are good for filling in small holes.

⑤ Tie a pretty piece of ribbon around the rim of the terra cotta pot. Fill the bottom of the pot, on top of the Styrofoam ball, with candies, and your centerpiece is ready to be, well, front and center!

Extra touch: For extra detail, you could paint or decoupage the terra cotta pot. Also, if you don't like the plain dowel, you could paint it, or cover it with ribbon or glitter!

Coffee-Can Ice Cream

You don't need a fancy freezer or a pricey pint of store-bought ice cream to enjoy a frosty sweet treat. A coffee can, some ice, and rock salt are all the "equipment" you need to whip up the basic makings of a great ice cream sundae party!

Project difficulty: Moderate (only because you may want an extra set of hands to help roll the coffee can!)

Materials

2 metal coffee cans, with lids, 1 can bigger than the other (for example, a 1-pound can and 3-pound can)

2 pints half-and-half

1 cup sugar

2 teaspoons vanilla

A bag of ice from the supermarket, or 2 large bowls of ice from your freezer

Rock salt (available at any supermarket)

Tools U Need

Wooden spoon or large mixing spoon

Strong tape, such as duct tape, masking tape, or mailing tape

DIY Step-by-Step:

1. Make sure both cans are clean and dry.
2. Put the half-and-half, sugar, and vanilla in the small can and stir them together. Put the lid on the can and make sure it is on tightly. Put a piece of tape across it to secure it.
3. Put the smaller can inside the larger can, centering it right in the middle. Around the smaller can, pack ice and rock salt, until the larger can is totally packed to the top. Put the lid on the larger can and secure it with tape.
4. Now, as silly as it might seem, roll the can back and forth for 30 to 40 minutes. You may want to put an old towel or blanket on the floor, sit on it with a friend, and roll the can back and forth to each other.
5. After at least 30 minutes has passed, open the large can and carefully remove the smaller can. Open the smaller can, and the ingredients should have frozen into a soft ice cream consistency!
6. If you'd like the ice cream to be harder, put the lid back on and tape it up again. Empty out the larger can, put the smaller can back in the center, and re-pack the large can with fresh rock salt and ice. Roll the can around on the floor for another 10 to 15 minutes, and the ice cream should be ready for eatin'!

Extra touch: If you want extra flavor right in the ice cream, stir in chocolate chips, diced fruit, nuts, or crumbled cookie pieces before you roll the can around on the floor!

Cookie-Cutter Finger Sandwiches

Everyone loves sandwiches, and these adorable little treats are not only yummy, but almost too cute to eat! Make bunches of them, in all varieties and shapes, for your party.

Project difficulty: Easy

Materials

Bread, any type

Sandwich makings (ideas: peanut butter and jelly; bologna and cheese; ham and cheese; turkey and cheese; plain cheese; peanut butter and marshmallow crème; cream cheese and jam; egg salad; tuna salad; peanut butter and honey; cream cheese and sliced veggies; or peanut butter and bananas).

Tools U Need

Cookie cutters, any shape and size you like

DIY Step-by-Step:

1. Make various kinds of sandwiches.
2. Place them on a flat surface and use the cookie cutters to cut shapes out of the whole sandwich, just as you would cookie dough.
3. Stack the cutout sandwiches on a bed of lettuce on a pretty platter.

Extra touches: Make little signs for the plates that tell what's inside each sandwich; on the serving plates, put little dishes of dipping sauce, like ketchup, mustard, mayo, onion dip, and hummus; use different types of bread for a variety of flavors and colors; line the mini sandwiches along the edge of your serving plate and fill the middle of the plate with chips, pretzels, cheese cubes, fruit, and crackers.

Edible Balloon Bowls

How do you make a bowl you can eat? The answer is: Chocolate! Isn't chocolate always the answer?

Project difficulty: Moderate

Materials

2 packages (12 oz. each) chocolate chips

1 package party balloons

Tools U Need

Large microwave-safe bowl

Wax paper

Baking sheet

DIY Step-by-Step:

1. Blow up several balloons about halfway and tie them off.
2. Cover the baking sheet with a sheet of wax paper and make sure there is room in your refrigerator to place the baking sheet.
3. Open the chocolate chips and dump them into the bowl. Microwave them for 30 seconds at a time, stirring in between each interval until the chips are totally melted. (Stirring is important—even after they're melted, the chips will hold their shape, and the chocolate will burn if you nuke it too long.) Let the chocolate cool slightly, for a couple of minutes.
4. Hold the balloon by the tied end. Dip the balloon into the chocolate and swirl it around for 10–15 seconds. The bottom fifth or so of the balloon should be covered.
5. Set the balloon on the baking sheet, and repeat with another balloon. Put the baking sheet with both balloons into the refrigerator for 15–20 minutes.
6. Remove balloons from the fridge and let them sit on the baking sheet for 5 minutes. Carefully pop the balloon and remove it from the chocolate . . . you have a chocolate bowl!
7. Reheat chocolate to create as many bowls as you need. Fill them with fruit, ice cream, other candy, mousse, or cake, and make sure you tell everyone they can eat the bowl!

Extra touch: You could use any kind of meltable chocolate for the bowls, including peanut butter chips or white chocolate chips (which you could then make into any color with food coloring).

Greeting-Card Ornaments

You won't believe just how pretty these ornaments are! Making them is fun, too, and they're perfect for any occasion as a party decoration, a party favor, or a project for a DIY party!

Project difficulty: Moderate

Materials

Several old greeting cards, any style—if you don't have old cards to cut up, ask friends and relatives or scour thrift stores, vintage shops, and 99-cent stores

Strong thread or fishing line

Tools U Need

Compass (or circle-shaped stencil)

Scissors

Pencil

Glue gun and glue sticks, or other strong glue

Ruler

DIY Step-by-Step:

1. Using the compass, a stencil, or another round object you can trace, draw 21 circles, exactly the same size, on the greeting cards (it will take several cards to get 21 circles; cut as many as you can from each card). A 2- or 3-inch circle makes a great ornament. Cut out all the circles.

2. Now, draw one triangle that will fit perfectly inside the circle. To do this, take one of the circles you just cut out and fold it in

half, then fold it into thirds. Unfold it, and make a mark with your pencil on the edge of every other fold. You should have three marks. Using the ruler, draw three straight lines connecting those marks, which should then form an equilateral triangle (a triangle that's the same length on all sides).

3 Cut the triangle out of the circle, and use it as a template. Trace it into the center of all 20 circles that you cut from the greeting cards.

4 Place one of the circles in front of you with the pretty side (the one with the decoration) facing up. On the triangle lines you drew, fold the sides of the circle up, toward the center. You should have a circle with three sides sticking up.

5 Repeat this process with the other 19 circles.

6 Pick up two circles, with the folded sides facing upwards, and glue one flap of one circle to one flap (it doesn't matter which one) of the other circle.

7 Continue gluing the other circles together, joining the flaps together with glue. You will begin to see a sphere shape form, and when all the circles are together, you will have a large, 3D ornament!

8 Make a small hole at the top of the ornament, tie a loop of fishing line through, and you're ready to hang your creations!

Extra touches: You could use any heavy stock paper for this project, including scrapbook paper or even junk mail! You can also add more decorative detail to the ornaments by tying ribbons around the top, adding glitter to them, or making a tassel to hang from the bottom of the ornament!

Piece of Cake

Here are nine quick ideas to make a boxed cake mix look and taste homemade!

1 Stir some extra taste into the cake batter: Chocolate chips, coconut, miniature marshmallows, and chopped-up candy bar bits all work well!

(continued)

2. When you're assembling a double-layer cake, put a surprise between the layers: Spread a layer of frosting on the bottom cake, then cover it with crumbled Oreos, mini M&Ms, chopped nuts, Nestle Buncha Crunch, or Nerds. Place the second layer on top, frost the entire cake, and sprinkle more goodies on top!

3. Stir fresh fruit—pineapple, blueberries, and raspberries work well—into a plain yellow or white cake-mix batter for quick flavor!

4. A plain yellow cake becomes an amazing strawberry shortcake when you cut it into little chunks, cover with fresh strawberries, and top with whipped cream!

5. Make a chocolate-cherry shortcake by cutting a plain chocolate or devil's food cake into small chunks, covering them with cherry pie filling, and topping them with whipped cream!

6. Make a cake mix much moister by adding a box of instant pudding mix to the batter before baking. Try matching up the cake mix with a complementary pudding flavor, like chocolate pudding with a strawberry cake mix, butterscotch pudding with a chocolate cake mix, or banana-cream pudding with a yellow cake mix.

7. When the boxed cake-mix instructions call for vegetable oil in the recipe, substitute an equal amount of applesauce instead. Not only will it make the cake healthier (less fat), it will also be moister. Bonus: Try a yellow cake mix with applesauce substitution, plus diced apples (without the peels) and cinnamon added to the batter. Yum!

8. Quick finishes to make a cake look like it came from a bakery: Sprinkle powdered sugar on top of a chocolate cake; sprinkle toasted or plain coconut on top of a frosted cake; press crushed walnuts along the side of a frosted cake; or put fresh fruit or pie filling between two round cake layers and frost the entire cake with whipped cream.

9. When making cupcakes, put a chocolate kiss or a mini peanut-butter cup in the middle of the batter before baking for a yummy melted treat when you bite into the finished cupcake.

Magazine Christmas Tree

These make great centerpieces for your Christmas in July (or Christmas in December) party!

Project difficulty: Easy

Materials

A digest-sized magazine, like *TV Guide* or *Reader's Digest*

Scraps of construction paper or other decorative paper

Tools U Need

Glue gun and glue sticks, or other strong glue

Scissors

DIY Step-by-Step:

1. Place the magazine on a flat surface, with the cover facing up.
2. Take the cover by the upper right corner and fold it down, toward the spine of the magazine. The folded part should form a triangle. Crease the fold down.
3. Take the bottom right corner of the page and fold it upward, until it meets the top fold.
4. Repeat the process with all the pages, until the entire magazine is folded this way.
5. When you stand it up and fan it out, the magazine will look like a mini tree! Glue the front and back covers together so the whole thing is round, like a real tree.
6. Cut out ornament shapes from various colors of paper and glue them on the tree. Make small garlands out of strands of beads, and glue them to the tree. Draw and cut out a gold star for the top!

Extra touch: You can spray paint the trees in gold or silver for a really cool look!

Party Blowers

What's a party without these festive favors? The best part about DIY
Party Blowers? You can make them out of any paper you want!

Project difficulty: Easy

Materials

Cool paper, like wallpaper scraps, scrapbook paper, or construction
paper

Drinking straws

Clear mailing tape

Tools U Need

Glue gun and glue sticks, or other strong glue

Scissors

Pencil

Rubber bands

Ruler

DIY Step-by-Step:

1. Cut strips of paper 2½ inches wide by 10 inches long.
2. Place a strip of paper on a flat surface, with the pretty side (the
   side with the design) face down.
3. Fold the long ends of the paper toward each other, so they meet
   in the middle. Put a strip of the clear tape down the middle of
   the strip, where the two folded sides of the paper meet.
4. At the short end of the strip (either short end), fold the paper
   over about ½ inch and seal it down with a piece of tape. It's
   important to make sure the end is taped down very well, so no
   air can get through and the Party Blower will work!
5. Starting at the end you just taped shut, begin rolling the strip of
   paper tightly around a pencil. When you're finished, carefully
   slip it off the pencil and wrap a rubber band around the roll to

make sure it stays tightly wound. Make as many of these as you need for your party, and let the rubber-banded strips sit for at least 10 hours.

6 Once the coiled strips have had a chance to set, take the rubber bands off. Fold in the corners of the open end, like a paper bag. Slip the end of the straw inside, about 2 inches. Put glue on the edges of the paper and fold them around the straw so that no air can get through between the straw and the paper (a small piece of clear tape may help seal the area more securely).

7 Let the glue dry for at least an hour. Test one of your favors—it should blow out and pop back into a roll each time!

Extra touch: Decorate the Party Blowers with glitter or stickers, or by personalizing them with each partygoer's name. You could also use multicolored straws, which are a great 99-cent store find.

6

DIY-a-Days

You never know when the mood to craft will strike . . . so these handy DIY-a-Day calendars (yep, there's one for every month of the year!) will ensure that you have an idea for something to do, make, read, or learn every single day of the year! There are also beauty tips, gift ideas, and recipes, as well as the birthstone, flower, and astrological sign for each month (all included to inspire more ideas for gifts and projects) . . . cool, huh?

DIY-a-Day: Get Crafty in January!

❀ This is the perfect month to brew a cup of flavorful tea, make the King's favorite meal, and start a new hobby!

January's birthstone is . . . Garnet

January's flower is . . . Carnation

January's astrological signs are . . . Capricorn (12/22 to 1/19) and Aquarius (1/20 to 2/18)

1 Happy New Year! Buy a plain journal or notebook, decorate it with stickers, fake flowers, or magazine cutouts, and write down your goals, plans, and wishes for the new year!

2 Brew a cup of flavorful tea—Celestial Seasonings Honey Vanilla Chamomile is yummy!—that does double duty as a tasty beverage and a fantastic potpourri!

3 It's Festival of Sleep Day. To help make sure you get a good night's sleep, put your blanket in the dryer for 5 minutes right before you hit the sack for toasty warm snoozing.

4 Celebrate National Trivia Day. Cruise Teenmag.com's celebrity trivia quiz section (go to *www.teenmag.com* and click the "Celeb Stuff" link), and make yourself an expert on your favorite stars!

5 Shop the post-holiday sales at Target, Kmart, craft stores, and other specialty and discount retailers for great supplies that you can use for next year's holiday DIY projects! Good post-holiday bargains: Christmas lights, tree decorations, wreaths, garland, almost anything red and green, beautiful holiday cards, wrapping paper, jingle bells, silk flowers, bows and ribbons, New Year's Eve party goods, holiday cookie cutters, and holiday music CDs.

6 Paint a small flowerpot with funky colors for a snazzy pencil cup.

7 It's Old Rock Day. Find a smooth rock, about the size of your fist. Paint cool patterns or flowers on it, and paint your name in the middle for a cool paperweight.

8 It's Elvis Presley's birthday. Celebrate with the king of rock 'n' roll's favorite food, the peanut-butter-and-banana sandwich. Spread PB on one slice of white bread. Slice half a banana and place it on top of the PB. Cover with another slice of bread and enjoy!

9 Today is National Apricot Day. Take one large can of apricot halves and puree them in a blender. Pour the mixture into an ice-cube tray, cover the tray with plastic wrap, and insert a toothpick into each cube. Place the tray in the freezer for 4–5 hours and enjoy your tasty apricotsicles!

10 Spend 5–10 minutes a day keeping your room neat and organized, which will save you from an hour or two of intense cleaning on the weekend!

11 January is National Hobby Month. Start a new hobby yourself! A few suggestions include crafts; reading; collecting stamps, books, photos, jewelry, rocks, dolls, stuffed animals, or something else that's important to you; photography; drawing; writing or keeping a journal; dancing; running; playing board games; learning a new language; and cooking or baking.

12 Gift-wrap idea: Use pages of your favorite magazines to wrap small packages, or crinkle them up and use them as packing material for inside the box when you're mailing a package!

13 National Poetry Day. Make up a rhyming poem about your favorite TV show.

14 Inexpensive crepe-paper rolls can be used for more than party streamers. You can use them as an alternative to ribbon when wrapping gifts!

15 Peanut butter spread on celery sticks is good. But add raisins or chocolate chips and you've got Ants on a Log!

16 Donate old books and magazines to your local library. If the library doesn't accept donations, try local elementary schools, shelters, and senior citizens' centers.

17 To get rid of dry, flaky skin on your hands, rub them with chilled coffee grounds. The grainy texture of the grounds helps slough off dry skin and helps get rid of the itchies!

18 January is National Staying Healthy Month. Start your day with a healthy smoothie each morning: Blend 1 banana with ½ cup of strawberries or blueberries plus 1 container of plain or vanilla yogurt, ¼ cup of ice-cold milk, and a couple of ice cubes.

19 It's National Popcorn Day! Make a big batch of microwave popcorn. As soon as the popcorn comes out of the microwave, while it's still hot, add in a package of M&Ms, some peanuts, a few small caramels, and some gummi bears or gummi worms.

20 Frame it: Glue starlight mints (you know, those red and white striped circle mints?) around a plain picture frame for a cool way to display your Yuletide pics!

21 Today is National Hugging Day. So let everyone you care about know by giving them a hug and a Hershey's Kiss!

22 Take an empty two-liter bottle of your favorite soda, cut a slot at the top of the bottle, and use it as your cool new coin bank. P.S.: Save your change all year and use it to throw a pizza party for you and your best buds in December!

23 It's National Pie Day. Instant Banana Cream Pie recipe: Crumble 2 large graham crackers into a dish. Cover with 1 Snack Pack container of vanilla or banana pudding. Slice one half of a banana on top of it and cover with Cool Whip. Mmmm!

24 It's Eskimo Pie Day! Try making your own frozen concoction by slicing vanilla ice cream into squares, inserting a Popsicle stick into the bottom, and dipping them in chocolate chips you've melted in the microwave!

25 Frame it: Collect a hodgepodge of buttons—different sizes and colors—and glue them to a plain picture frame for a room decoration that's, y'know, cute as a button!

26 Wash your hair and braid it while it's still wet. Let the braids dry naturally—this is a good trick to try before you go to bed at night—and when you undo them, your hair will have at least twice the body as usual.

27 January is National Thank-You Month. Say thank you to some-one special with this simple DIY gift: Tie a handful of colorful lollipops, like Chupa Chups, Dum Dums, Tootsie Roll Pops, or Blow Pops, together with a pretty ribbon for a cool candy bouquet.

28 National Kazoo Day! Make your own kazoo by wrapping a piece of wax paper around one end of an empty paper towel or bathroom tissue roll. Tape it into place and hum into the open end of the tube for some crazy kazoo-like sounds.

29 Frame it: Paint an inexpensive picture frame black and glue dominoes all around it for a great way to display a black and white pic!

30 When laundering a load of bright clothes, put a tablespoon of salt into the wash cycle. It will keep the colors from run-ning, especially in new clothes!

31 It's National Scotch Tape Day! Celebrate by visiting the 3M (makers of Scotch Tape) Web site (at *www.3m.com*) to find free patterns you can print out to make your own gift boxes.

DIY-a-Day: Get Crafty in February!

❀ Looking for ideas for Valentine's Day goodies, how to make your own kite, and . . . Snow Ice Cream??? *Really*, it's yummy!

February's birthstone is . . . Amethyst

February's flower is . . . Violet

February's astrological signs are . . . Aquarius (1/20 to 2/18) and Pisces (2/19 to 3/20)

1 February is International Friendship Month! Write a letter to a friend—even someone you see at school every day. Decorate the envelope with markers and stickers. Wouldn't you love to get a surprise like that in the mail?

2 A few drops of your favorite perfume added to a plain lotion equals custom-made body lotion.

3 Save colorful juice or iced-tea bottles to use as vases for a single flower.

4 It's National Wild-Bird Feeding Month. Take a saltine cracker, spread both sides with peanut butter, roll it in birdseed, and string it on a tree by threading string through the cracker holes. A tasty treat for your feathered friends!

5 DIY Gift: A cool cookie cutter, with your favorite cookie recipe printed on a colored index card and attached to the cutter.

6 Find cookie recipes for every taste: *www.allhomemadecookies. com* or *www.allrecipes.com.*

7 Cut a lemon in half and rub one half on each of your elbows to get rid of dead skin.

8 Today is Kite Flying Day! So . . . go fly a kite! If you want to make your own, like the one Benjamin Franklin used for his

famous experiments, check out the PBS Web site (go to *www.pbs. org/benfranklin/exp_kite.html*).

9 Frame it: Glue candy hearts around a plain photo frame for the perfect place to display the pic of the person you ♥ most!

10 It's Umbrella Day. Spruce up an old umbrella—or buy an inexpensive and plain new one—and paint it with permanent markers!

11 Snow (only very, very clean, fresh snow!) plus 1 cup of milk plus ½ cup of sugar plus 1 teaspoon of vanilla equals Snow Ice Cream! P.S.: If you can't find a patch of super-clean snow, make your own with shaved ice.

12 Yum, it's International Pancake Day! Make your breakfast cakes extra special by adding in chocolate chips, chopped nuts, coconut, chopped-up candy bars, or food coloring (who wouldn't want pink or purple pancakes???).

13 Instead of buying valentines, make one for each person on your Valentine's Day card list. Use pretty red, pink, and purple papers, lace, ribbons, paper doilies, markers, stickers, and beads, and handwrite a personal message on each one.

14 Happy Valentine's Day! Make a special Valentine's Day gift: Cover a dozen Oreos in melted chocolate. Add some red sprinkles, cinnamon hearts, red gummies, conversation hearts, and messages you write with frosting. Let them dry, and wrap them in a pretty box with pink or red tissue paper and tie with a ribbon.

15 Make a regular cup of hot cocoa special by adding in a Hershey's Kiss, a chocolate mint, or a candy cane to stir it!

16 Send a secret message: Dip a toothpick, cotton swab, or paintbrush into lemon juice and write your message on a piece of

white paper. Once it's completely dry, hold it up to a light bulb. The heat from the bulb will make the message "magically" appear!

17 For super-effective hair conditioning, comb your favorite conditioner through your hair and leave it on. Cover your hair with Saran Wrap and leave the conditioner on for 15 minutes. Rinse with cool water, and notice how much softer your hair is!

18 Sew two pretty washcloths together, leaving a small opening. Stuff with fabric fill or cut up pantyhose, stitch the opening, and you have a cool terrycloth pillow. Make a bunch for your bed!

19 February is National Grapefruit Month. Try this super yummy treat for breakfast or for dessert: Preheat the oven to 350 degrees. Cut a grapefruit in half. Place both halves, face up, on a cookie sheet. On each half, sprinkle 2 tablespoons of brown sugar and 1 tablespoon of butter. Bake in the oven for 7–8 minutes, until sugar and butter have melted, and enjoy!

20 Instead of painting a really old chest of drawers, why not decoupage it with photocopies of your favorite pictures or lots of colorful Sunday comics?

21 Shoeboxes covered with wrapping paper, colorful Sunday comics, magazine pages, or fabric make great—and thrifty!—storage containers.

22 It's National Cherry Month. Fill an ice-cube tray ¾ of the way to the top and pop a maraschino cherry in the middle of each cube. Freeze for a colorful addition to water, iced tea, or ginger ale.

23 Use office labels and markers, colored pencils, watercolors, or crayons to make your own stickers.

24 Crush your old eye shadow into white nail polish for a groovy new nail color.

25 When you pack your brown-bag lunch today, pack enough for two and surprise your best bud with a lunchtime picnic!

26 It's National Snack Food Month! Bake a batch of cupcakes or cookies and surprise your friends with a lunchtime snack that will definitely beat anything the cafeteria is serving!

27 Take a plain hatbox, or recycle an old one, paint it, and trim the top and bottom with a matching ribbon or fringe.

28 Wash your hair with warm water—it helps open the follicles and lets the shampoo and conditioner really work—but do your final rinse with cool water, which helps bring out the shine.

29 (In case it's Leap Year!) Use aluminum foil as gift wrap. Finish the package with a bright red ribbon or bow.

DIY-a-Day: Get Crafty in March!

✿ And learn ways to celebrate National Oreo Day, make your own envelopes, and create a matching necklace and bracelet set that is as tasty as it is fashionable!

March's birthstone is . . . Aquamarine

March's flower is . . . Daffodil

March's astrological signs are . . . Pisces (2/19 to 3/20) and Aries (3/21 to 4/19)

1 It's National Peanut-Butter Lover's Day. Wanna make your own? Put 1 cup of roasted peanuts (out of the shell, of course) in a blender, along with 1½ teaspoons of peanut oil. Blend on medium speed until the mixture is the consistency of paste and spread it on a slice of bread for a taste test!

2 Frame it: Glue multicolored gumballs around a plain photo frame.

3 Before applying lipstick, run an ice cube over your lips. The cold helps set the lipstick and prevent it from smudging and wearing off throughout the day.

4 Try this unique way to display your artwork or your favorite magazine pin-ups: String clothesline from corner to corner across the walls of your room, and hang the pages with clothespins or large paper clips. Bonus: The sheets are easily changed, for quick redecoration whenever the mood strikes you!

5 Make your own envelopes out of magazine pages, wallpaper, newspaper, wrapping paper, or other foldable materials. Take an existing envelope and gently open its seams to use it as a template. Trace the template onto your paper, and use the template's folds as a guide to folding your new envelope. Seal with glue stick.

6 It's National Oreo Cookies Day—yum! One small flowerpot (washed and lined with wax paper or plastic wrap) plus crushed Oreos (which will look like dirt) plus gummy worms and gummy bugs equals an edible pot of dirt 'n creepy crawlies!

7 Make a designer-esque watch. You can usually find cheapie watches for $2 or $3 at a discount store. Buy one and hot glue crystals or cool beads to the band.

8 Here's an inexpensive makeup remover: baby shampoo!

9 Happy birthday, Barbie! Barbie was officially "born" in 1959. Quick wall art: Paint a simple wood frame. Mount one of your old Barbie doll outfits (or score some from a yard sale, Goodwill, or closeout store) on a piece of background paper, and put it in the frame. Group several together on your wall for a cool display!

10 Super-fast drying method for freshly painted fingernails: Dip your tips into a bowl of ice-cold water!

11 March is National Youth Art Month. Visit a museum. Take a mental picture of your favorite artworks, and recreate one of them for your bedroom wall.

12 Make Rice Krispies Treats (the recipe is on the Rice Krispies box), but instead of cutting them into squares, use cookie cutters to cut them into cool shapes.

13 More Rice Krispies Treats tips: Follow the same recipe, but substitute Fruity Pebbles, Froot Loops, or Cocoa Pebbles for the Rice Krispies. Or use a mixture of two or three of the cereals for a funky Treat.

14 It's National Potato Chip Day. Try this: Instead of dip, dunk your plain potato chips in ketchup. It may sound weird, but it's just as tasty as ketchup on French fries! Really!

15 Frame it: Glue small pretzels around a plain, inexpensive photo frame to make a hotspot for one of your favorite pics.

16 Make fruit kebobs by cutting pineapple, watermelon, apples, grapes, cantaloupes, and strawberries into chunks and putting them on Popsicle sticks.

17 Happy St. Patrick's Day! Make green cupcakes; put green food coloring in your Sprite or water; wear a green scarf, beret, or hair band; paint your fingernails green; and hang a big green shamrock cut out from posterboard on your locker.

18 It's the anniversary of the first time a man walked in space. How about making some homemade moon pies? Spread marshmallow crème between two graham crackers, and dip the sandwich in melted chocolate. Chill them in the refrigerator for 2–3 hours and prepare yourself for an out-of-this world flavor!

19 DIY Gift: Using your favorite refrigerated cookie dough (or a recipe for your favorite homemade cookies), cut slices of the roll of dough, place them on a cookie sheet, and before you pop them into the oven, put a Popsicle stick or lollipop stick into the cookie. When the cookies are baked and cooled, wrap them with colored plastic wrap, tie several together with a ribbon, and voila: cookie bouquet!

20 It's National Quilting Day. Check out SoYouWanna.com's How to Quilt section. Go to *www.soyouwanna.com* (and click the "SYWs A to Z" link, where you'll find "quilting" under "Q") for a complete tutorial on how to get started with this very, very cool art form.

21 March is National Craft Month. Start your own crafts club at school!

22 Christmas may be nine months away, but a string of bright lights will still look way cool hanging around the mirror in your bedroom.

23 To keep your eyebrows in line, spray a small bit of hairspray on an old toothbrush or brow brush and sweep it across your brows.

24 Hooray for National Chocolate-Covered Raisins Day. Sure, you could buy some Raisinettes to celebrate. Or you could celebrate the DIY way by covering raisins in melted chocolate. Bonus: Try covering them in melted white chocolate, too.

25 Today is National Waffle Day. Skip the maple syrup, and try some new toppings on your waffles: fresh strawberries and whipped cream; peanut butter, jam, or jelly; powdered sugar; chocolate chips, chocolate syrup, caramel syrup . . . the possibilities are endless!

26 Make an edible necklace: Take a strand of string licorice (long enough to fit around your neck) and thread Froot Loops, Apple Jacks, jelly rings, Life Savers, round gummies, and other ring-type foods you can think of on the licorice, tie a knot at the end, and wear! (Then eat!)

27 Make an edible bracelet to match yesterday's necklace!

28 It's National Something-on-a-Stick Day. To celebrate, make a Frozen 'Nana On a Stick. Take one banana, skewer with a Popsicle stick. Cover it with melted chocolate chips and then roll in crushed Oreos. Place on a sheet of waxed paper and freeze for three hours . . . yummy!

29 No shaving cream in the shower? Use your hair conditioner to make your legs a slick canvas for shaving.

30 Cover a Styrofoam ball with fake flowers. (Cut the stems off, leaving just enough to stick the flower into the Styrofoam.) Fashion a loop by tying a piece of ribbon, and hot glue the ribbon loop onto the Styrofoam for a very cool flower ball. This makes a great party decoration or just a groovy conversation piece hanging from the ceiling in your bedroom.

31 It's National Frozen Food Month. Make your own pudding pops: Add 1 box of instant pudding (any flavor) to 2 cups of cold milk, and mix well with a fork. Pour into ice-cube trays, small paper cups, or other small molds and place a Popsicle stick or toothpick into the center of each one. Freeze for at least 5 hours, remove from molds, and savor the flavor!

DIY-a-Day: Get Crafty in April!

❀ Make a cool bank to save all your pennies (and nickels and dimes and cash of the paper variety!) and make over a plain watch!

April's birthstone is . . . Diamond

April's flowers are . . . Sweet pea and Daisy

April's astrological signs are . . . Aries (3/21 to 4/19) and Taurus (4/20 to 5/20)

1 April Fool's! Fool your friends with this yummy recipe. Bake a batch of cupcakes . . . in ice cream cones! Place cones in cupcake tray. Fill cones halfway with cake batter and bake according to directions on package. When done, cover with frosting and sprinkles, just like a real ice cream cone!

2 It's National Peanut-Butter-and-Jelly Day. Take a plain flour tortilla, spread it with peanut butter and your favorite jelly, roll it up, and nuke for 15 seconds. Yum!

3 DIY Gift: Using a black marker, draw simple shapes, one to each page, on sheets of white paper. Examples: fruits, houses, animals, flowers, trees, fish, books, cars, clothes, etc. Make 15–20 pages, design a cover page, staple them all together, and give your favorite crayon artist a personalized coloring book!

4 Cool gift bag: Put gift inside a plain brown paper bag, and gather the bag closed at the top. Tie with a pretty ribbon, and write a message directly on the bag. Especially handy for disguising irregularly shaped gifts!

5 Press fresh flowers by placing them between two sheets of wax paper and placing them in the middle of a heavy book. Let dry for several weeks and make beautiful cards with them!

6 Buy a pair of cheapie rubber boots at Target or Payless, and paint cute flowers or designs on them in funky colors. Make sure you use waterproof paints or paint markers—available at craft stores.

7 DIY Gift: For a sick friend or family member, buy a mini teddy bear from a craft store and put a cool neon or other funky Band-Aid on the bear. Attach a personal get-well message and let your loved one know you're wishing him or her a speedy recovery!

8 Frame it: Glue Legos, toy cars, or little plastic soldiers around an inexpensive picture frame.

9 Glue jigsaw puzzle pieces to the top of plain office-supply push-pins for some groovy additions to your bulletin board.

10 It's National Humor Month. Make up your own knock-knock joke.

11 Decoupage inexpensive votive candleholders with magazine pictures or pretty floral pics from bridal mags and flower catalogs.

12 Buy a cheap watch and replace the cheesy band with a strip of beautiful grosgrain ribbon.

13 It's National Garden Month. Make your own Chia Pet by cracking an egg at the top carefully, making sure the bottom half of the shell is intact. Remove all the egg insides, and fill the intact half-shell with potting soil. Sprinkle a few grass seeds on top of it, and push the seeds into the soil. Do this with a bunch of eggs and store them in the egg carton, with the lid closed, checking them periodically to make sure the soil is moist. In a couple of weeks, your egg will start to sprout green "hair." Draw a face on the shell and name it before you give your egg pet a haircut!

14 It's Income Tax Day. That means your parents are probably way stressed out. And since April is also National Stress Awareness month, surprise the 'rents with a special gift: Hugs and Kisses. Fill a mug or small gift bag with Hershey's chocolate Hugs and Kisses, along with a real hug and kiss, of course!

15 Instant coin bank: Wash an empty Pringles can and cover the outside with pretty paper. Place the lid on top, cut a slot in the lid, and start saving that cash!

16 Buy a cheapo straw bag from a discount store, or even a yard sale, and make it look like a million bucks by hot gluing a gorgeous silk flower to the front and wrapping the handles with a matching color of ribbon.

17 Spruce up a pair of plain socks by adding fabric trim, ribbon, pom-poms, googly eyes, or even inexpensive rhinestones (all goodies available at a craft store) with fabric glue.

18 DIY Gift: A stress ball! Using a funnel, fill a colorful balloon with sand or cornstarch, stretching the balloon gently to get the filled ball to the size you want it, and then tie it off. P.S.: The stress ball should be small enough to fit in one hand.

19 Need a cool headboard for your bed? Mark off a rectangle above your bed with masking tape or another removable tape that won't leave residue on your wall. The rectangle should be as wide as your bed and as tall as you want. Fill the space with a collage of your favorite celeb pin-ups, your favorite ads, CD covers, or magazine covers!

20 DIY Gift: Make a mix CD for a friend, and wrap it with a piece of photocopied sheet music (you can find sheet music at your local library).

21 It's National Jelly Bean Day! Eat a few of these super sugary candies, and then make a picture out of some. Separate the beans by color, sketch a simple design on a piece of paper, and use the jelly beans as "paint" to fill in the picture by color. Glue them down and hang your nifty artwork.

22 Today is Earth Day. Find out how you can do your part to keep our planet in tip-top shape by visiting the Kids section of www.Earth911.org.

23 Yum, it's National Pigs-in-a-Blanket Day. Preheat the oven to 375 degrees. Open a can of refrigerated biscuits. Cut a hot dog in half. Cut a cheese slice in half. Place a cheese slice on one of the biscuits, top it with one of the hot dog halves, and roll the biscuit closed, like a hot dog bun. Place the "piggies" on a cookie sheet and bake in the oven for 10–12 minutes.

24 Store your candles in the freezer when you aren't using them. It will make them burn longer when you do!

25 It's National Pretzel Day. Take the salty snack food for a new spin by dipping them in peanut butter, jelly, onion dip, melted cheese, melted chocolate chips, salsa, sour cream, frosting, or ranch dressing.

26 Make your own "border tape" for your room: Simply make photocopies of all your favorite photos, cut them to the same size, and tape them along your wall side-by-side!

27 Take a plain pillowcase and spruce it up by using fabric glue to decorate it with felt cutouts (polka dots or hearts are always good!).

28 It's National Zipper Day. Know how to unstick a stuck zipper? Rub soap, a candle, or even a white crayon on it.

29 April is Keep America Beautiful Month! Plant something.

30 April showers bring May flowers . . . so get your vase ready! Or make one by taking an old drinking glass or an inexpensive fish bowl and decorating it with a paint marker.

DIY-a-Day: Get Crafty in May!

❀ May is a good month to decorate your computer, make Tootsie Roll earrings, and learn how to spruce up a plain glass of water . . . read on!

May's birthstone is . . . Emerald

May's flower is . . . Lily of the valley

May's astrological signs are . . . Taurus (4/20 to 5/20) and Gemini (5/21 to 6/21)

1 It's National Hawaiian Lei Day. Make your own lei by stringing inexpensive craft store flowers on embroidery thread, or, for a fresh lei, string carnations!

2 Tired of a plain computer monitor? Frame your monitor with colorful Post-It Notes.

3 It's American Bike Month. Cut colorful straws (the neon ones are the best!) all the way down, length-wise, and put them on your bicycle tire spokes.

4 Crushed eye shadows or blush plus a dab of Vaseline equals a custom-made lipstick. Store in an empty lip-gloss pot, and apply with a small makeup brush.

5 DIY Gift: Personalized washcloths or dishcloths. Buy inexpensive, plain washcloths and dishcloths at Target or Wal-Mart, and spruce them up by sewing pretty trim or ribbon around the edges.

6 Buy plain, inexpensive gift bags (they're often two or three for a buck at 99-cent stores!) and personalize them with cutout flowers, magazine cutouts, drawings, stickers, ribbons, and pieces of fabric. That cheapo bag will look like something you'd pay $6 or $7 for in a gift shop!

7 Take a pair of empty earring hooks (available at any craft store), and put them through cute, colorful wrapped candies, like baby Tootsie Rolls or Starbursts. You'll have a pair of unique accessories that can be changed as often as you like (not to mention a quick snack at the end of the day!).

8 It's National Have-a-Coke Day. Have your Coke in a glass filled with two scoops of cherry or vanilla ice cream, for a vanilla Coke or cherry Coke float!

9 Today is National Cartoon Day. Create your own comic strip based on the funniest person you know.

10 Use sparklers (only if they're legal where you live!) instead of candles to top a birthday cake.

11 Half a cup of baking soda plus ¼ cup of water equal a great hair revitalizer that will bring back the shine and take away the shampoo buildup from your tresses.

12 Know someone with a cast on an arm or leg? Decorate it for them with markers, stickers, or even decoupage with magazine cutouts!

13 It's National Tulip Day. Just a few flower stems wrapped in pretty tissue paper and tied with a matching ribbon will cost under $5 and will look like an expensive flower-shop bouquet.

14 It's Marshmallow Fluff Day. Make a classic fluffernutter sandwich by spreading marshmallow fluff on one slice of bread and peanut butter on another slice. Put them together and . . . yum!

15 Frame it: Use old game-board pieces—Scrabble letters or Monopoly money, for example—to decorate a plain photo frame. Glue the Scrabble letters around the frame, or decoupage the frame with the Monopoly bucks!

16 DIY music-maker: Peel the label off an empty 20-ounce soda bottle and fill it with rice, small macaroni noodles, or small pebbles. Decorate with stickers or magic markers and shake, shake, shake a tune!

17 Black Forest Dump Cake: Pour 2 cans of cherry-pie filling into a rectangular baking dish. Pour 1 package of dry chocolate cake mix over the top of the cherries. Cut 1 stick of butter into slices and dot them across the top of the cake mix. Bake for 45 minutes in a 375 degree oven, let cool, and serve.

18 It's Older Americans Month. Go out of your way to do something special for a grandparent or other older person you know.

Offer to mow a lawn or help with housecleaning chores, or, best of all, give your most valuable resource—your time—by visiting with an older neighbor.

19 Wrap pretty and soft chenille pipe cleaners around your pens and pencils . . . it looks cool and provides a nice little cushion for your fingers.

20 It's National Egg Month. For shiny hair, mix a raw egg with a handful of shampoo and wash and rinse your hair as usual.

21 Replace the shoestrings in your sneakers with pretty ribbon.

22 DIY Gift: Cut four 12 × 12 inch squares of pretty, colorful felt fabric. Out of the felt scraps, cut flowers, squares, circles, and other simple shapes. Arrange the cutouts on the 12 × 12 inch squares and glue them down with fabric glue. Let them dry, roll each square up, and tie it with a piece of ribbon. Put four together in a box with tissue paper for a cool set of napkins!

23 Cut lemon slices and orange slices and put into glasses of water and diet soda for an extra twist.

24 It's National Pickle Week. Make your own dill pickles: In a clean jar, pack 6 stalks of dill weed, 1½ tablespoons of sugar, 3 tablespoons of salt, ½ cup of cider vinegar, and several small to medium-sized unpeeled cucumbers. Fill the jar to the top with cold water and put the lid on tightly. Put the jar in the refrigerator and let sit for 4 weeks. One month later: tasty goodies!

25 Open a roll of refrigerated sugar or chocolate chip cookie dough, and add your own goodies for extra special treats. Suggestions: M&M's, walnuts, Hershey's Kisses, pecans, Reese's Pieces, miniature peanut-butter cups, crushed candy canes, Nerds, and marshmallows.

26 May is National Physical Fitness and Sports Month. Instead of joining a pricey gym, start your own exercise club with friends. Take walks together, jump rope, play tennis, swim, shoot hoops, or check out an aerobics tape from the library. Most importantly, find ways to exercise that are also fun, so you'll want to make being active a regular thing!

27 Make your own beautiful dried flowers and use them in art projects or to make your own cards. Just press the flowers (smaller ones like daisies and buttercups work best) between two sheets of waxed paper (or two coffee filters) and put them between the pages of a very heavy book, like a telephone directory or an encyclopedia. In two weeks, they'll be dried and ready to make something pretty!

28 National Hamburger Day, yum! Instead of a regular hamburger, shape your burger into a hot doggish link and cook it that way. Serve it in a hot-dog bun with ketchup, mustard, and even a little relish.

29 Once a month, clean your combs and hairbrushes by removing all the loose hair, and soak them in a sink or bowl filled with hot water and a few drops of shampoo.

30 Have a sports-themed room? Use a hockey stick as an alternative to a curtain rod.

31 May is National Photo Month. When you finish a mirrored compact of makeup, don't throw the container away. Remove the tray that held the actual makeup, and cut a photo to fit into the space. Decorate the outside with beads, fabric flowers, or magazine cutouts, and you'll have a personalized mirror/picture frame for your purse!

DIY-a-Day: Get Crafty in June!

❀ Frozen grapes? Recycled Etch-A-Sketches and Lite Brites? And a day that celebrates everything pink? It's all part of the DIY goodness of June's DIY-a-Day line-up!

June's birthstone is . . . Pearl

June's flower is . . . Rose

June's astrological signs are . . . Gemini (5/21 to 6/21) and Cancer (6/22 to 7/22)

1 It's National Doughnut Day! Preheat an oven to 350 degrees. Cut a plain doughnut in half and spread cherry pie filling on one half. Put the two halves together, put the doughnut on a cookie sheet, and put more cherry pie filling on top. Put the sheet into the oven for 10–12 minutes. Remove from the oven, and let it cool. Right before you're ready to eat it, put a scoop of whipped cream on top and sprinkle with chopped nuts!

2 Recycle an old Etch-A-Sketch (or find a gently used one at a yard sale, secondhand store, or vintage shop) by using it as a picture frame. Simply cut a photo to fit the size of the screen and glue it on!

3 June is National Zoo and Aquarium Month. Plan a trip to your local zoo, take lots of great pictures, choose your favorites, and make a calendar with them.

4 Buy a paint-by-number kit and make a new artistic masterpiece for your room.

5 Pop some grapes in the freezer for a couple of hours for a chillingly good treat.

6 DIY Gift: Doodad Jars. Take a clean Mason jar—or another clean, empty jar that you've moved labels from—and fill with little treasures: pennies, charms, colored dice, bits of ribbon, pretty

hair clips, small plastic animals, little party favors, bits of tinsel, bits of colorful confetti, pretty wrapped candies, small toys with special meanings, and so on. Cover the top of the jar with a piece of fabric, put the lid on and then tie with a nice ribbon. Make a personalized tag that tells the recipient that each item in the jar is good for one wish!

7 It's yummy National Chocolate Ice Cream Day. Two Chips Ahoy cookies plus 2 tablespoons of softened chocolate ice cream equals a yummy and quick ice cream sandwich!

8 It's Best Friends Day. Write a song about your best friend, print it on a cool sheet of paper, roll it up, tie it with a ribbon, and give it to your bud. Better yet, make a tape recording of you singing the musical tribute to your friendship!

9 Easy nightstands for your room: Turn a cheap plastic wastebasket or garbage can upside down and put a piece of sturdy wood—which doesn't even need to be painted—on top of it. Cover the whole thing with a large piece of fabric (a pretty, inexpensive bed sheet will work) and make a matching one for the other side of the bed!

10 June is National Iced-Tea Month. Make a jar of sun tea. Get a large glass jar (enough to hold 1 gallon of water). Fill it almost to the top with cold water and float four to five tea bags in the jar. Put the lid on and find a sunny spot—a windowsill, the porch, or right out in the yard—and let the tea "brew" until it's a medium brown color. Add sweetener, if you like, along with ice cubes and lemon slices, and enjoy.

11 Here's a fabulous, unique piece of jewelry that's guaranteed to cost you no more than a buck: the Dollar Bill Ring! Using nothing more than a $1 bill and a simple bit of origami, you can have a very cool ring. Check out *www.pallerfinancial.com/ringinst.htm* for complete instructions!

12 It's National Peanut-Butter Cookie Day. Try this recipe for no-bake PB cookies: Crush 2 cups of graham crackers and add them to 2 cups of powdered sugar, 1 cup of peanut butter, and 1 cup of melted butter. Spread that mixture into a large baking pan. Melt 1¼ cups of chocolate chips and pour that over the mixture in the pan. Put the pan in the refrigerator for 2 hours, and cut into squares (or any other shape you like!) before eating.

13 Whoops, it's National Juggling Day! Learn to juggle on *www. Juggling.org*.

14 Happy Flag Day. Make a groovy American flag pillow. Cut out two rectangular pieces of white felt, whatever size you desire (14 inches × 10 inches makes a nice pillow for your bed or a sofa). With wrong sides facing outward, match up the rectangles and use fabric glue or simple sewing stitches to secure the fabric together, leaving a small hole for stuffing. Turn the pillow right side out, stuff with batting or old panty hose, and sew or glue shut. On the front: Glue strips of red felt, leaving alternating strips of white. In the upper left corner, glue a piece of blue felt to the pillow, and glue rows of small white buttons, or white stars you've cut out of extra white felt, to the blue area.

15 Use scarves as curtain tiebacks.

16 Find a pretty silk flower, paint the edges with glue, and dip it in glitter. Use hairpins to wear it in your hair!

17 It's National Eat-Your-Vegetables Day! Plain celery sticks are boring. Try adding cream cheese, peanut butter, or even salsa to them for souped-up veggies!

18 It's International Picnic Day. Pack your own outdoor feast in a basket or backpack: sandwiches (get fancy and cut the crusts off!), crackers, squares of cheese, pretzels, celery with peanut butter, frozen grapes, cookies, water, soda, and mints, plus plates, utensils,

napkins, cups, and a pack of baby wipes for quick cleanup. Bonus tip: Freeze some juice boxes ahead of time, and pack them with the other goodies. They'll not only keep the other food cold, but they'll slowly thaw just in time to be a refreshing beverage!

19 Buy plain headbands (they're usually available in bunches at 99-cent stores) and decorate them with ribbons, beads, rhinestones, fake flowers, and glitter.

20 National Ice Cream Soda Day. Ice cream sodas . . . they're not just for root beer! Add 1 cup of your favorite soda to 2 scoops of vanilla ice cream for a frosty treat that's good, no matter what flavor you choose!

21 Need a lamp for your room? Plug in a Lite Brite toy instead!

22 You've heard of duct-tape wallets, right? How about a duct-tape evening gown?! Check out the official Duck Tape Web site at *www.ducktapeclub.com* and click the "Contests" link for all the details on how you could win a scholarship by making a DIY dress with the sticky stuff.

23 Hooray, it's National Pink Day! Wear a pink outfit, drink Cherry 7-Up, put pink carnations in a vase in your room, use only a pink pen to write, wash your hair with strawberry shampoo, make pink cupcakes for your family and friends, chew pink bubblegum, listen to a Pink CD, sleep in pink jammies, eat Frankenberry cereal for breakfast, have pink lemonade for lunch, and paint your fingernails—you guessed it—pink!

24 Make a crafty necklace by hooking together colored paper clips! For an even fancier result, "string" small beads on the paper clips before hooking them together.

25 Make a matching paper clip bracelet for yesterday's necklace.

26 It's yummy National Chocolate Pudding Day. Make a no-bake chocolate cream pie: Prepare two boxes of instant chocolate pudding as directed on the box. Pour the pudding into a graham cracker piecrust, top with Cool Whip, and chill in the refrigerator for at least an hour.

27 Half a cup of lemon juice plus 3 tablespoons of baking soda plus 2 teaspoons of liquid soap mixed together and spread on hair for 30 minutes after you get out of the swimming pool equals clean, shiny hair that doesn't smell like chlorine.

28 A clean ice-cube tray makes a great jewelry box for earrings, rings, necklaces, and other small treasures. Find trays in cool colors at discount stores, and personalize them by adding ribbon, trims, or fake rhinestones around the edges!

29 It's National Camera Day. Would you believe you can make your own camera with an oatmeal box, a soda can, and some glue? You can! Check out this oatmeal-box pinhole photography Web site (*http://users.rcn.com/stewoody/*) for the scoop!

30 Here's an idea for unique carpeting in your room: Have a patchwork carpet! Go to your local carpet store and ask them if you can buy scraps of various carpets (you should be able to save lots of cash, too). Take them home, measure your floor, and cut squares from the scraps to fit the measurements!

DIY-a-Day: Get Crafty in July!

✿ It's summer and it's hot, but here are 31 cool ideas (sorry for the pun!) to keep you craftin' throughout the month!

July's birthstone is . . . Ruby

July's flower is . . . Larkspur

July's astrological signs are . . . Cancer (6/22 to 7/22) and Leo (7/23 to 8/22)

1 DIY Gift: When giving a gift certificate, make the presentation extra special with the "wrapping." Put a movie certificate inside a box of microwavable popcorn or a box of movie candy; for a music certificate, slide the paper inside a mixed CD you make especially for the recipient!

2 Afraid your breath has that not-so-fresh smell? Try chewing a sprig of fresh parsley.

3 Make a fabulous Fourth of July dessert: blueberry and cherry or strawberry Jell-O. Once they're chilled and firm, spoon a layer of the red Jell-O into a dish, followed by a layer of whipped cream, then a layer of the blue Jell-O. Top it all off with a big, juicy strawberry!

4 Happy Independence Day! DIY Gift: Fill a glass jar with one layer of red jelly beans, one layer of white jelly beans, and one layer of blue jelly beans, and tie with red, white, and blue ribbon and a mini flag.

5 Make cool gift tags with origami techniques. Check out *www.paperfolding.com* for instructions.

6 DIY Gift: Design a cool border using photos, cartoons, drawings, clip art, cool fonts on the computer (spell out the recipient's name in script, for example) on a sheet of paper. Go to a Kinko's or other copy shop, and have them copy the design onto 25 sheets of paper. Add 25 blank sheets and matching envelopes, and tie it all together with a ribbon for a personalized stationery set.

7 Mmmmm, it's National Strawberry Sundae Day. Go all strawberry: Put 2 tablespoons of strawberry syrup or jam in a small bowl. Put 2 scoops of strawberry ice cream on top. Cover with 2 more tablespoons of strawberry syrup or jam, and add ½ cup of sliced strawberries on top of that. Top with 1 tablespoon or 2 of whipped cream, and end with a sprinkling of strawberry-flavored Nerds!

8 Today is National Video Games Day. Set up your own video game tournament with friends and make it a party with snacks, music, and a crown (made with gold-colored posterboard adorned with fake rhinestones) for the champion!

9 Makeup brushes should be cleaned at least once a month, by soaking them in baby shampoo.

10 Frame it: Glue various colors of dice around a plain picture frame. Make this a gift for a loved one who loves Las Vegas!

11 When using curling mousse or gel in your hair, apply it when hair is soaking wet and scrunch it throughout your locks.

12 Instead of searching for the perfect swimsuit, buy a plain one and make it perfect yourself! Pick a plain suit you like and that fits well, and sew colorful buttons (craft stores have plastic buttons shaped like everything from fish to rubber duckies!) and a pretty ribbon trim on it.

13 Take a plain, inexpensive long mirror (maybe there's one stored away in the garage or attic? If not, they're usually available at Target or Kmart for about $10), paint the frame, and hot glue fake flowers, a feather boa, fake leaves, pinecones, beads, pom-poms, or other trims around the frame.

14 DIY Gift: A plain laundry bag can become a great gift for a friend or relative (or yourself!). Cut out a bunch of flowers or other simple shapes from various colors of felt, and hot glue or simple stitch them to the bag.

15 Bagel cut in half plus ¼ cup of tomato sauce plus shredded cheese plus pepperonis or veggie strips plus toaster oven or regular oven equals your own personal pizza!

16 Use a favorite photo, or make a collage of your faves, and print them out on a sheet of iron-on transfer paper. (This can also

be done at a copy shop like Kinko's.) Iron onto a pillowcase or onto several pillowcases for a matching set!

17 Natural hair lightener: Mix water and lemon juice in a bottle and spritz it onto your hair before going into the sun.

18 A simple letter becomes an amazing treasure when you present it in a cool envelope that's decorated with markers and stickers.

19 Start your own Web site! Check out Webmonkey for Kids (go to *www.hotwired.com* and click the "Webmonkey Kids" link) for a complete lesson on Web site building, along with ideas and tools to help you become part of the information superhighway!

20 Super-Easy Fudge: Pour a bag of chocolate chips and a can of condensed milk into a microwavable glass bowl and nuke for 2 minutes. Stir, and cook at 1-minute intervals until the mixture is well blended. Pour into a glass baking dish and chill in refrigerator until fudge is set. Optional add-ins: nuts, marshmallows, or gummi bears.

21 Raining outside? That's the perfect excuse to have a picnic inside, right on your living room floor!

22 Today is National Hot Dog Day. Try it Chicago-style: Put your hot dog on a poppy seed bun, topped with tomato slices, pickles, onions, and celery salt. It may sound weird at first, but there's a reason it's a classic in the Windy City!

23 Quick table for your room: Make three to four equally tall stacks of books (hard-covers are sturdier), and arrange them in a triangle or square. Put a piece of glass or sanded and painted wood on top, and you've got a table. Place some throw pillows around the table and make it your hang-out area when friends come over!

24 It's National Virtual Love Day. Tell someone you love how much he or she means to you via e-mail or instant messaging!

25 Today is National Threading-the-Needle Day. A quick tip for threading a needle: Lick the end of the thread to make it stiff before you try to thread it through the hole.

26 Sunburn soother: Run a warm bath and pour 2 cups of buttermilk under the running water. Use a moisturizing lotion on your skin when you get out of the bathtub.

27 DIY Gift: Confetti Crayons. Take broken crayons, or even pieces of broken crayons, of all colors and make a whole new drawing tool! Remove wrappers from crayons and put them together in a microwavable cup. Nuke on high for 4–5 minutes, stirring them every 45 seconds or so. Once crayons are totally melted, remove the cup (using a potholder or towel!), and pour the mixture into a mold or a cookie cutter. Let it cool. Wrap your creations in plastic wrap and tie with a ribbon, or arrange several different Confetti Crayons in a small box, nestled in tissue paper.

28 Want striped walls but don't want to pay hundreds of dollars for fancy wallpaper? You can achieve the same look by using a ruler, a pencil, and masking tape to mark off stripes on a wall and paint "around" the stripes.

29 Paint an old stool and use it as a small table for your bedroom.

30 One can of sweetened condensed milk mixed together with one can of frozen lemonade and one tub of Cool Whip, then poured into a graham cracker piecrust and chilled equals a Five-Minute Lemon Cream Pie.

31 To write a special message in icing on a cupcake or birthday cake, put frosting into a zip-close bag, seal the bag, smush icing into one corner, cut a tiny snip off the bag, and you've got a cool piping tool!

DIY-a-Day: Get Crafty in August!

✿ Make your own bubbles, recycle Dad's ugliest tie for a cool belt, and pay homage to the ice cream sandwich in August.

August's birthstone is . . . Peridot

August's flower is . . . Gladiolus

August's astrological signs are . . . Leo (7/23 to 8/22) and Virgo (8/23 to 9/22)

1 Frame it: Glue little paper beverage umbrellas around a plain frame for a cool place to show off your vacation photos!

2 Today is National Ice Cream Sandwich Day. Make an ice cream sandwich buffet with several kinds of cookies, two or three flavors of ice cream, and tiny chocolate chips, sprinkles, and chopped nuts. Put a scoop of ice cream between two cookies, smush together, and roll in one of the toppings!

3 It's National Watermelon Day. Cut a fresh, juicy watermelon into chunks or use a melon baller to cut it into convenient little bite-size globes. Pop them into the freezer for an hour, and enjoy a frosty treat that's as refreshing as ice cream (and way healthier!).

4 One cup of dishwashing liquid plus 2 cups of water equals bubble solution! Store your mixture in an empty film container, and bend a pipe cleaner into a small circle to use as a bubble wand.

5 Need a quick gift bag? Cut the top off an empty cereal box. Punch two holes at the top in the front and the back of the box. String yarn or another strong cord through the holes to make handles, line the box with a sheet of tissue paper, and put your present inside!

6 Save the coffee grounds from your parents' morning pot of java. Mix them with water in a baking pan (preferably a disposable one), and soak sheets of white paper in the mixture. After several hours, remove the paper and let it dry for a cool, parchmenty kind of look.

7 Make a windsock: Take an empty oatmeal container or milk carton and discard the tops (for the carton, cut the spout part off). Cover with cool paper or plain paper you've decorated. Punch 6–8 holes all around the bottom with a knife, and thread a piece of ribbon, colorful string, or crepe paper through each hole. At the top, punch two holes (on opposite sides). Thread a strong piece of ribbon or rope through them, and tie them off to make a hanger. Tie it to a tree, your mailbox, or a porch and wait for a gust of wind to make it fly!

8 DIY Gift: A Candy Pot. Paint a flowerpot with bright, multicolored shapes. Fill it with licorice sticks, candy sticks, and lollipops.

9 Doughnuts on a Stick: Make or buy plain doughnuts. Insert a Popsicle stick in each one, dip in melted chocolate chips or cake frosting, and top with colored sprinkles or chopped nuts.

10 It's American Artist Appreciation Month. YOU are an American artist, so get out those watercolors, colored pencils, crayons, markers, and collage materials and make yourself a masterpiece!

11 Want a cheer-y look for your bedroom windows? Hang a cheerleading pom-pom at each end of your curtain rods.

12 Pronto Pineangel Cake: Mix one box of angel food cake mix with one large can (about 20 ounces) of crushed pineapple (with the juice). Spread mixture into a sheet cake pan, and bake at 350 degrees for 30 minutes. Serve with vanilla ice cream or whipped cream . . . Mmmmmmm!

13 DIY Gift: Collect—from discount stores, vintage shops, garage and yard sales, or flea markets—beautiful teacups and saucers (they don't have to match!). Melt and pour candle wax into a teacup, insert a wick, and let it dry. Set the cup on a saucer, place them in the center of a sheet of plastic wrap or tissue paper, gather the paper, and tie with a ribbon.

14 August is National Foot Health Month. Try this great-smelling recipe for getting your tootsies baby smooth: Mash 12 strawberries with 3 tablespoons of olive oil. Put your feet into the bathtub and spread the mixture all over your feet. Massage the mixture in for 5–10 minutes, and rinse it off.

15 Today is National Garage Sale Day. Have a garage sale or yard sale of your own. You get rid of clutter and you might just make a few bucks, too (all the better to buy more junk!).

16 Need a nifty belt? Ask your dad or grandfather if you can raid their closets for old ties, which you can thread right through the belt loops on jeans, shorts, and skirts. Or shop at vintage and secondhand stores for funky, colorful ties.

17 It's National Thrift Shop Day. When you visit a thrift shop, look for things—especially really inexpensive items—that you might be able to "makeover" into something else. Examples: An old scarf might become a cool belt . . . an old lunchbox might become a cool purse . . . a plain old fabric tote bag may have designer-like possibilities if you dye it and add colorful beads and replace the handles with cool ribbon!

18 Scribble away, it's National Pencil Day. Choose a color of pencil that you like best, and make it your "signature" pencil. Only use that color of pencil and make it extra cool by tying a ribbon around the top, or twirl one of your hair scrunchies around it!

19 Today is National Potato Day. Make a yummy meal out of those leftover mashed potatoes by making Potato Pancakes! Mix an egg into the leftover potatoes and then divide the potatoes into equal amounts and shape them into hamburger-sized patties. Pat just a bit of flour on each side of the patty and fry it in a buttered frying pan until each side is crispy brown. Drain the Potato Pancakes on a paper towel, and enjoy with ketchup, salsa, sour cream, or applesauce!

20 Make a batch of No Bakes, the world's greatest cookie (really!). In a large saucepan, heat 1 stick of butter, ½ cup of milk, 4 heaping tablespoons of Hershey's cocoa powder, and 1 cup of sugar. Stir occasionally, and, over medium heat, let the mixture come to a boil. Immediately remove the pan from the heat, and stir in 3½ cups of oatmeal and ½ cup of peanut butter. Stir the mixture until all the ingredients are well combined. Then, drop tablespoons of the mixture onto waxed paper and let them cool. After about an hour, the cookies should be cooled and set and ready to eat!

21 It's National Friendship Week! DIY Gift: Make a "What I Like About You" Jar! Cut sheets of 8½ × 11 inch paper into 30 strips (so there's one for every day in the month), in various colors. On each strip of paper, write one thing you like about your best friend. Take an empty, washed baby-food jar, jelly jar, or other small glass jar and remove the labels completely. Fill the jar with the message strips, tie with a pretty ribbon, and make a label that instructs the recipient to read one special thing about herself or himself each day!

22 A storage trunk—a cool vintage one from a flea market, maybe from your grandparents' attic, or an inexpensive one you can buy at Target or Kmart—not only makes a great storage unit for the end of your bed, but can also do double duty as a little table. If it's a sturdy trunk, you can also put a cushion or pillows on top and use it as a bench!

23 Put your moisturizer in the refrigerator overnight for a super cool and refreshing feeling in the morning, especially in the summer!

24 One box of brownie mix (prepared as directed on the package) plus 1 cup of coconut flakes, chopped nuts, mini M&M's, or chocolate chips added to the batter equals brownies with a twist!

25 Make a collage out of old magazines, but only use one color.

26 Today is National Cherry Popsicle Day. Fill an ice-cube tray with cherry Kool-Aid. Place a real cherry in the middle of each cube. Cover with plastic wrap, and insert a toothpick through the wrap and into the center of each cube. Put into the freezer until set, and enjoy!

27 It's Make Your Own Luck Day. Give everyone you know a lucky penny to carry around for the day!

28 Fun picnic dessert: Serve ice cream sundaes in small (unused) beach sand pails. Eat them with the shovel that came with the pail!

29 Yummy toast topper: peanut butter sprinkled with a mixture of cinnamon and sugar.

30 It's National Inventor's Month. Do you have an idea for a great invention you'd like to make? Check out the Wild Planet Toys Web site for a chance to do just that with the company's annual Kid Inventor Challenge (*www.kidinventorchallenge.com*)!

31 DIY Gift: Wash an empty pint ice cream container (like Ben & Jerry's) and insert a gift certificate from your favorite ice cream shop, or make a certificate that entitles the recipient to a homemade ice cream sundae . . . made by you, of course!

DIY-a-Day: Get Crafty in September!

✿ Among September's bright ideas: Throw a back-to-school bash for your friends, turn your old junk into new cash, and cure your tummy flip-flops with lemon!

September's birthstone is . . . Sapphire

September's flower is . . . Aster

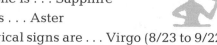

September's astrological signs are . . . Virgo (8/23 to 9/22) and Libra (9/23 to 10/22)

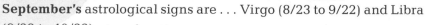

1 It's National Library Card Sign-Up Month. If you don't already have a card, sign up for one. Browse the crafts books section and pick a new craft or hobby to learn!

2 Use a scarf to tie your ponytail.

3 Throw a back-to-school DIY party for your friends.

4 Gift wrap idea: Use colorful Sunday comics, and tie your package with a big red bow!

5 Decoupage a plastic bangle bracelet with candy wrappers, like Starburst or Blow Pops.

6 Need another bracelet to match your outfit? Tie a pretty piece of fabric ribbon in a bow around your wrist.

7 Use fabric softener sheets as odor busters in your shoes. Insert one sheet into each shoe and leave them overnight.

8 Turn your unwanted clothes into someone else's treasure while making yourself some cash for new duds. How? Consignment shops will sell your gently used goods and give you a percentage of the profit. Find one near you at *www.consignmentshops.com*.

9 It's National Teddy Bear Day. Show your teddy bear love with a makeover: Tie a new ribbon on it, use one of your bracelets as a necklace for it, tie a scarf around its neck, and put one of your old hats on it.

10 Before serving hot food, soak your plates in warm water in the sink. Helps keep your tasty dinner hot longer!

11 Today is National Make-Your-Bed Day. Make sure you'll have a relaxing sleep at night by spritzing your sheets and pillowcases with some homemade linen spray: Mix 15 drops of lavender-scented essential oil with 1 cup of water, and put it in a spray bottle. Lavender helps your whole body relax!

12 YUM, it's National Chocolate Milkshake Day. Here's a recipe for a simple (and simply delicious!) chocolate milkshake: 1 generous scoop of your favorite chocolate ice cream plus 1 cup of whole milk plus 3 tablespoons of chocolate syrup, mixed in a blender. For extra flavor: add 2 Oreos, a couple of chocolate chip cookies, 2 tablespoons of chocolate chips, 4 miniature Reese's Cups, half a small bag of M&M's, or half a box of Junior Mints!

13 Store a spoon in the refrigerator overnight. Hold the cup part over your eyes for a few moments in the morning for a refreshed look and a quick cure for puffy eyes.

14 It's National Coupon Month. Make your own coupons and pass them out to friends and family. (See the sidebar on page 38 for ideas!)

15 Make your own soda by mixing your favorite juice with plain seltzer water.

16 DIY Gift: Homemade soaps or great-smelling soaps you purchase at drugstores, discount stores, or bath-and-body shops become special gifts when you individually wrap them in pretty tissue paper and tie them with ribbons and faux flowers.

17 Cool bookmark: Cut a strip of pretty ribbon about 12 inches long. Tie a knot at one end. At the other end, tie a knot about a third of the way down. Then string seven or eight cool beads and tie another knot at the end. The beaded end will hang over your book while the rest of the ribbon marks your place!

18 National Playdough Day. Try this super-scented version of homemade dough: Cinnapple Playdough. Mix 1 cup of cinnamon with 1 cup of applesauce until it makes a doughy substance (you may have to add a tiny bit more cinnamon to get it to the correct consistency). This wonderful smelling dough is great for making little sculptures that will continue to smell great even after you let them dry for a day or two!

19 It's National Deaf Awareness Week. Learn the basic American Sign Language alphabet—go to *www.lessontutor.com/ASLgenhome.html*.

20 A capful of mouthwash in your shampoo once a week helps fight dandruff.

21 Spray paint a glass soda bottle and let it dry. Once it's dry, brush it with a thin layer of glue and roll it in glitter. Put a single flower in it, and you have a fancy new vase.

22 September is National Sewing Month. DIY Gift: Sew two pieces of square fabric together (wrong sides facing each other), leaving a small opening for stuffing. Turn right sides out and fill with old pantyhose, socks or fabric stuffing. Sew opening closed and decorate by gluing random—the more mismatched in color and size the better—buttons to the front in a random pattern. For a more personalized gift, spell out the recipient's name in buttons!

23 Line the inside of an empty Pringles can with plastic wrap or a plastic grocery bag. Wrap can with wallpaper, gift wrap, yarn, ribbon, or plain white paper you've decorated with markers or watercolors . . . instant vase!

24 Make an old coffee table or end table into a permanent art canvas by priming it and then painting it with blackboard paint (yep, it turns the surface into a chalkboard!). Bonus: Cover an old coffee can or tin can with cool paper and fill with chalk for when the inspiration to draw on your new table hits you!

25 Today is National Comic Book Day. Pick your favorite comic book and write and illustrate a story with your favorite characters!

26 It's National Pancake Day. Make Pancake Roll-Ups for a portable breakfast. Spread pancakes with peanut butter and jelly, roll them up, and sprinkle with powdered sugar. An alternative: Spread a thin layer of applesauce and powdered sugar on the pancake before rolling it. Or, if you're more of a traditional pancakes-and-syrup fan, roll up a plain pancake and dip it in the syrup!

27 Mash ½ avocado with 2 tablespoons of plain yogurt. Smooth onto face and let sit for 15 minutes. The result: smooth, soft skin.

28 Decoupage your bedroom light switch plate with magazine pages, wrapping paper, or the cover of an old paperback book!

29 A cheap, but colorful alternative to fresh flowers: Find interesting-looking twigs, and spray paint them any color you like. Arrange them in a cool vase or a large glass bowl.

30 An upset stomach leaving you feeling a little queasy? Cut a fresh lemon in half and smell it. The powerful citrus odor "tricks" your brain into forgetting that your tummy isn't feeling so swell.

DIY-a-Day: Get Crafty in October!

❁ Boo! It's Halloween month, so check out this DIY-a-Day roundup for ideas on costumes, decorations, and, of course, yummy tricks and treats!

October's birthstone is . . . Opal

October's flower is . . . Marigold

October's astrological signs are . . . Libra (9/23 to 10/22) and Scorpio (10/23 to 11/21)

1 It's National Homemade Cookies Day. Shape the entire batch of cookie dough into one giant cookie! When baking the single monster cookie, baking time will be longer, and it's important to check it frequently to make sure it's not undercooked or burnt! Decoration tip: Draw hearts or a personal message on the super cookie with frosting.

2 Using mini pumpkins, make individual Halloween treats for everyone in your fam'. Write their names in glue on a pumpkin, then sprinkle the glue with black, green, or gold glitter. Make one for each person in the family, and use them throughout the month as special name cards each night at dinner.

3 October is National Pizza Month. Make a pizza bar for friends or family: Slice English muffins and bagels in half. In small bowls, set out pizza sauce, pepperonis, shredded mozzarella cheese, chopped onions, chopped green peppers, pineapple, cooked ground beef, chopped olives, sliced barbequed chicken, and any other cool pizza topping you can think of. Have each person top their own mini pizzas and bake them in a 400 degree oven for 7–9 minutes each.

4 DIY Halloween costume: Blow up 100 purple balloons; wear a plain dark sweatshirt and sweatpants; tape the balloons to your shirt and pants. You're a bunch of grapes! Bonus tip: Ask several friends to wear the same costume . . . you're a bunch of bunch of grapes!

5 Using pretty paper, make an accordion fold fan (by folding a paper, lengthwise, back and forth) and tie a matching ribbon at the bottom. Make several and hang them in your room.

6 It's National Apple Month. Set up an apple bobbing game! Fill a large bucket or tub with cool, clean water, and then place 8–10 apples in the water. Everyone gets a turn leaning over the bucket and trying to "catch" an apple in their teeth. Remember: No fair using your hands to help you get an apple.

7 Can't find a lint brush to make your coat or sweater free of pulls? Make your own: Loop a piece of tape around your fingers with the sticky side up and brush it against your garment!

8 DIY Halloween costume: Wear brown shorts, brown tights, a brown T-shirt or sweatshirt, and a yellow scarf around your neck. Wrap your torso in aluminum foil, leaving part of your shirt and the scarf exposed . . . you're a baked potato (with butter)!

9 Fill a short, plain glass bowl with many different colors of marbles for a simple centerpiece for your dresser.

10 Make your own business cards (standard business card dimensions are 2 × 3.5 inches)! Design your own on the computer and print them on colored cardstock, or, for something really different, cut the cardstock to size, and hand-print each card!

11 Super fall treat: Haystacks! Melt a bag of chocolate chips in the microwave, stir in 1 cup of chopped pecans and 1 cup of crunchy chow-mein noodles. Form mixture into little balls, and let them cool on wax paper.

12 Today is National Farmer's Day. DIY Halloween costume: A pair of overalls plus a plaid shirt, straw hat, and a stuffed animal cow or pig . . . you're a farmer!

13 Want filing cabinets in your room but hate the boring old industrial-steel gray color of office-supply store cabinets? No prob! With a coat of primer and the fabulous paint color of your choice, you can have groovy cabinets to match the rest of your room! Bubblegum pink filing cabinets? Can do!

14 Make a personal "coffee table book" of photos for a friend, using an inexpensive photo album, photocopies of your fave pics, and captions that you write yourself!

15 Cut the ends off a Twizzler and use it as a straw.

16 It's National Dictionary Day. Look up a new word each day in the dictionary. Keep a list of all the words you learn.

17 DIY Halloween costume: Wrap your entire body with a few inexpensive rolls of first-aid gauze (make sure you don't cover your nose, mouth, or eyes, of course, and wrap your legs individually so you can still move!) . . . you're a mummy! Bonus tip: Carry a baby doll with you, add a wig and draw lipstick on the gauze around your mouth . . . you're a mommy mummy!

18 October is National Clock Month. Make your own clock! Buy a clock parts kit at any craft store, and insert it into the hole of an old record album! Other ideas for cool clocks: an old DVD or CD (especially those free AOL discs!), record album cover, photo, old tote bag, basket, cereal box, or even a magazine!

19 It may require a bit of time to initially organize, but consider putting your CD collection in alphabetical order by artists' last name. It will make finding your favorite tunes a snap!

20 DIY Gift: Decoupage pics of flowers from a flower or seed catalog or empty seed packets to a terra-cotta pot. Once dry, put several new packets of various flower seeds and a pair of gardener's gloves inside and tie a ribbon around the pot.

21 Frame it: Make the perfect fall frame by gluing leaves, acorns, or tiny plastic pumpkins around a plain frame.

22 DIY Halloween costume: Wrap your entire body with rolls of orange crepe paper (again, wrap your legs individually, and don't cover up anything you need to see or breathe with!) . . . you're a cheese doodle!

23 October is National Family History Month. Make a family tree, write letters to out-of-town family members, or help plan a big family reunion.

24 Make a groovy birthday-cake card: Take a blank sheet of cardstock, fold it in half, and glue several real birthday candles to the top. Draw a cake or cupcake for the candles to stick into, and draw flames on top of the candles!

25 Today is National Denim Day. Take your least-favorite pair of jeans and turn them into your favorite: Sew ribbon trim around the bottoms of the legs and down each side along the legs.

26 Blackhead buster: Mix baking soda and water until it forms a paste. Spread on your face, using a circular motion, with your fingertips, for three minutes. The graininess of the mixture helps remove the blackheads.

27 DIY Halloween costume: Cover yourself with an old white sheet (cut holes for eyes, nose, and mouth) and carry around a pencil cup with pens, pencils, and markers in it . . . you're a ghost writer!

28 You and your pals feeling a little too, ahem, mature, for trick-or-treating this year? You're never too old for the treats part, so surprise your friends with a little goody bag of orange and black sweet treats, including orange gum, black licorice whips, orange slices, circus peanuts, and orange and black jelly beans!

29 Design a logo for your name!

30 Yum, it's National Candy Corn Day. DIY Halloween Gift: Take a plain white paper cup, and paint the bottom ⅓ yellow, the middle ⅓ orange, and leave the top ⅓ white, so the cup looks like a piece of candy corn! Fill the cup with REAL candy corn—and other holiday treats—wrap it in plastic wrap and tie with orange and black ribbon!

31 Happy Halloween! Wrap a white tissue or a square piece of white tissue paper over the top of a Tootsie Roll Pop. Tie a piece of ribbon or string around the "neck" (where the lolly meets the stick) to secure. Draw eyes and a smile (or a scowl!) with a pen . . . voila, a Lollipop Ghost! (And a great goody for the trick-or-treaters!)

DIY-a-Day: Get Crafty in November!

❀ Highlights of November's DIY-a-Day: how to tame hair frizzies, decorations to make for your family's Thanksgiving celebration, and ideas for a tasty way to put those Turkey Day leftovers to good use!

November's birthstone is . . . Topaz

November's flower is . . . Chrysanthemum

November's astrological signs are . . . Scorpio (10/23 to 11/21) and Sagittarius (11/22 to 12/21)

1 Got a pizza or pasta sauce stain on your shirt? Rinse it with cold water, pour white vinegar on it, and then rinse the vinegar out with more cold water. Wash the shirt as you normally would.

2 Gift wrap idea: Use old maps!

3 Empty Jell-O and pudding cups are perfect for holding paint when you're working on your next masterpiece.

4 DIY Gift: A personalized water bottle. Buy an inexpensive plain clear bottle (available at discount retailers like Target and Wal-Mart) and thoroughly wash it with hot, soapy water. Decoupage it, cover it with fabric, beads, ribbons, and trim or paint it with paint markers and stickers, making sure not to get any materials near the opening, so it's still safe for drinking.

5 Make your own jigsaw puzzle: Paste a magazine page or small poster to a piece of heavy cardboard (like posterboard or a cereal box front). Once the photo is dry, cut it into several pieces, with each piece a different shape. Make it as difficult or easy as you like, and store it in a pretty colored envelope. P.S.: These make great gifts for smaller children! Use pictures of their favorite cartoon characters.

6 Frame it: Glue checkers around a plain frame for a cool, unique way to display your favorite photos.

7 Spritz your hairbrush with hairspray before you brush with it to help tame static flyaway hair.

8 DIY Gift: Spray paint a large terra cotta flowerpot. Let it dry. Then decorate by gluing beads randomly all over the pot and fabric trim along the top edge. Completely cover the inside with plastic wrap and fill the pot with bananas, apples, oranges, grapes, walnuts in the shell, and cinnamon sticks. It's a Pot o' Fruit!

9 Frame it: Got a cool picture of your pet you'd like to display? Glue animal crackers, small dog bones, or little cat toys around a plain picture frame.

10 Keep a Wish Book, a journal of all the things you hope to see, do, own, be, buy, sell, or make some day. Write stories and cut out pictures of places you'd like to visit; crafts you'd like to try; skills you'd like to learn; the clothes, books, cars, houses, etc., you'd like to own some day; adventures you'd like to go on; the people you'd like to meet; the kind of person you want to be; your college and career goals . . . think of it as a "catalog" of you!

11 Plan a craft night with your family!

12 Puffy eyes? Close your eyes and put a cool cucumber slice on each eye.

13 Make your family dinner a festive occasion: Cut out cool shapes—hearts, stars, snowmen, turkeys, or pumpkins, for example—and write each person's name on one. Decorate with ribbons, glitter, and markers, and place them beside their plates at dinner!

14 Recycle an old stepladder. Paint it white, and decoupage pictures from a flower catalog on it. Then place plants, stuffed animals, or collectibles on each step for a unique display stand.

15 If you have a paper shredder in your house, make your own cool gift bag filler. Shred magazine pages, junk mail, construction paper—anything that has a lot of color—and use it to pack boxes and your holiday goodie bags!

16 Skin-softening bath oil: Mix 1 cup of baby oil with ¼ cup of essential oil in the aroma of your choice.

17 Make a craft "apron" to protect your clothes from paint and other supplies by taking a large garbage bag and cutting holes for your head and arms.

18 Soak a cotton ball in your favorite perfume or scented oil. Cut two small scrap pieces of felt, put the soaked cotton ball between them, and glue the felt pieces together. Make several and put them in the bottom of your trashcan, in a corner at the bottom of your closet, or in the bottom of your dresser drawers for a great scent. (Just be careful not to put the sachets against any delicate fabrics . . . you don't want to stain your favorite clothes!)

19 Make a grade-school–style construction paper turkey by tracing your hand (remember, your thumb is the turkey head!).

20 Want a fancy cosmetic bag? Buy a plain, inexpensive one and "write" your name on it with glue. Sprinkle glitter where the glue is, or cover glue with rhinestones or crystals for a super cool, designer-like, personalized bag. Bonus tip: The bag could also be used as a tiny purse, pencil case, or a change bag.

21 Cut off the top and half of one of the short sides of a cereal box—pick one that has a front that you like or that will look cool in your room . . . instant magazine holder!

22 Most shampoos are actually much stronger than they need to be to get your hair clean. Make your favorite shampoo last longer by pouring half of a new bottle into an old bottle that has been thoroughly cleaned. Mix cold water into each one until the bottles are full and shake them very well. Voila: two bottles for the price of one!

23 Quick snack: Spread cream cheese on a piece of ham and roll it up! If you're more into veggies, try cream cheese on a piece of celery.

24 Collect paint sample cards from a hardware or paint store. Arrange them into a cool collage, mount it on a piece of posterboard, and hang in your room.

25 DIY Gift: Make your own book-and-tape sets for your favorite preschooler. Buy a great storybook—all the Dr. Seuss books are a good bet—and make a cassette recording of you reading the book! Bonus tip: Use books your favorite tyke already has, and read several of them on one tape. Make a cool label for the cassette and call it your little friend's "Greatest Hits."

26 Combine 2 tablespoons of honey and 3 tablespoons of heavy whipping cream for a soothing, moisturizing facial mask. Spread it on your face, massage into your skin for a few minutes, and rinse with warm water, then cool water.

27 Refresh a worn or vintage button-down shirt by putting all new buttons on it.

28 Today is National French-Toast Day. Mix 2 eggs (beaten), 1 cup of milk, and 1 teaspoon of vanilla. Cut 3 slices of bread in half from top to bottom, then cut those halves in half the same way. Soak the bread sticks in the egg mixture, then fry in butter in a frying pan. Cook well on both sides, and when crispy brown, drain the sticks on a paper towel. While still hot, sprinkle them with powdered sugar, and dip in syrup or jam!

29 Looking for a way to gobble up some of that leftover Thanksgiving turkey? Make your own tasty and toasty quesadillas! Preheat the oven to 400 degrees. Place one burrito wrap flat on a piece of aluminum foil. Cover it with chopped or sliced turkey, shredded cheese, and chopped onions and green peppers, then add another thin layer of shredded cheese. Put another burrito wrap on top. Place the quesadilla on a cookie sheet and bake at 400 degrees for 12–15 minutes (check to see that the cheese is fully melted). Carefully remove it from the oven, and cut it like a pie into several pieces. Garnish with sour cream, salsa, and more shredded cheese.

30 Frame it: Glue Mike & Ike candies, M&Ms, Skittles, or Starburst (in the wrapper) around a plain picture frame for a sweet place to show off a picture of your sweetie!

DIY-a-Day: Get Crafty in December!

✿ And to celebrate the holidays, here's a DIY-a-Day calendar filled with ideas for holidays gifts you can make, delicious DIY treats, and groovy decorations that will help fill everyone you know with the spirit of the season!

December's birthstone is . . . Turquoise

December's flower is . . . Holly

December's astrological signs are . . . Sagittarius (11/22 to 12/21) and Capricorn (12/22 to 1/19)

1 Dip the bottom half of unwrapped candy canes in melted white chocolate chips, and cover in holiday colored sprinkles or crushed candy canes.

2 DIY Gift: Using sheets of magnetic backing (available at office supply stores), make personalized magnets with photos of family and friends, magazine cutouts, catalog pics, or your own designs.

3 Make paper snowflakes with different colors of paper, and decorate the family fridge or your bedroom door.

4 DIY Gift: Instead of making a single mix CD, why not make four or five and give your own personalized box set? Make the set a theme: all love songs, all dance music, each disc devoted to one artist, all TV theme songs, each disc a movie soundtrack, and so on.

5 Make a construction paper garland—you know, the kind you used to make in grade school. Cut strips of paper, loop them around each other, and staple or glue them together into a chain.

6 DIY Gift: A great gift for a friend or loved one who likes to bake—fill each well of a muffin tin with different small candies or snacks (candy hearts, sprinkles, mini chocolate kisses, mini M&M's, colored sugars, Goldfish crackers, crushed Oreos, and so on). Wrap the entire tin in cellophane or plastic wrap and tie with a ribbon.

7 Buy plain Christmas ornaments and write a name or a design on them with glue. (Tip: A pencil eraser dipped in glue makes a perfect dot!) Sprinkle colored glitter or tiny beads over the glue for a very cool, handmade heirloom.

8 DIY Gift: Find children's wooden blocks with the letters of the alphabet on them (this is a good discount store or 99-cent store find). Find the letters to spell out the name of a friend or loved one, line them up side by side, and glue them together with a glue gun or a strong glue made for wood. Instant nameplate for a desk!

9 String popcorn with a needle and thread and hang it on the tree. For extra color, string a cheap plastic bead, a cranberry, a Froot Loop, or a jellybean between each kernel of popcorn! Bonus tip: Make smaller strings of goodies and wear them as holiday necklaces!

10 DIY Gag Gift: Snowman Poop! Put a handful of mini marsh-mallows in a plastic bag and seal it with a tag that says "I hear you've been naughty, so here's the scoop: I'm out of lumps of coal this year, so you're getting Snowman Poop! Love, Santa."

11 Decorate a plain pair of gloves by sewing mini silver jingle bells to the wrist.

12 DIY Gift: This is a great one for a baseball fan! Find out the fan's favorite team and what the team's colors are. Paint a base-ball in those colors!

13 Paint pine cones white. When dry, paint random pieces of the cone with glue and dip them in gold glitter.

14 DIY Gift: Don't forget your favorite pooch or the beloved pet of a friend or family member at the holidays! A simple recipe for Peanut Butter Pooch Pastries: Preheat your oven to 350 degrees. Mix 2 cups of flour with 1¼ cups of milk, 1¼ cups of peanut but-ter, and 1¼ tablespoons of baking powder together in a large bowl. Once ingredients are thoroughly mixed, spread a thin layer of flour on a counter and roll the dough out to about a ½-inch thickness. Use a cookie cutter to cut shapes. Place cookies on a cookie sheet and bake for 17–20 minutes, until the tops of the cookies start to turn crispy brown.

15 Holiday decorating or centerpiece idea: Make your own snow globe! Check out *www.ehow.com*, and type in "snow globe" in the Search box for complete instructions!

16 DIY Gift: The family recipes! Gather favorite recipes from everyone in your family—including parents, grandparents, aunts, uncles, cousins, siblings, and close family friends. Type each recipe into a layout program on the computer, along with the name of the person who submitted it, and a story or quote from that person about why that recipe is a favorite. Add clip art and pictures (or wait to add art by hand once they're printed). Print out all the pages, design a cover, punch three holes down the left side of the pages, and tie a ribbon through each one. Print out many copies, and give one as a gift to everyone who contributed a recipe. Alternative idea: Print the recipes out on colored index cards and package them in a small, decorated box.

17 Make thank-you notes to send to family and friends after the holidays.

18 DIY Gift: Buy a dozen pairs of decorative socks, or buy a dozen pairs of plain socks and decorate them with ribbons, beads, small flowers, and so on. Package them in an egg carton (one pair rolled up to fit in each hole), and decorate the top of the carton with the recipient's name.

19 Suggest to friends that you have a Secret Snowflake gift swap. Bonus tip: Make the gift exchange even more interesting by setting a limit on how much everyone can spend—see who can come up with the best gift for $5 or $10! Or agree that all the gifts have to be homemade!

20 DIY Gift: Buy a package of pretty colored plastic spoons (craft stores have many different colors available) and a bag of meltable chocolate discs. Melt the chocolate in the microwave, and dip spoons into the chocolate until the "cup" part of the spoons are covered. Let the spoons cool, cover the chocolate part with plastic wrap, and tie with a pretty ribbon. Spoons are great for stirring extra flavor into hot cocoa or coffee.

21 Gather friends and family and go caroling in your neighborhood, to a senior citizen center, or to a hospital.

22 DIY Gift: A stocking full of stocking stuffers! Instead of one big gift, fill a stocking (or a really cool sock!) with several small gifts: some cool pencils and erasers, a bottle of nail polish, stickers, individual packets of hot cocoa, candy sticks, hand lotion or bubble bath, hair clips, tiny stuffed animals, earrings, Hershey's Hugs and Kisses . . . and any other small goodies you can find!

23 Make individual gingerbread houses for everyone at your holiday dinner table. Gather small milk cartons (the kind they serve in school) for each person at the table. "Glue" graham crackers to the outside of the cartons with frosting, one cracker on each side, and then two slanted crackers to form the roof of the house. Continue decorating the house with frosting (white frosting on the roof will look like snow!), gum drops, and candy canes. Use small frosted wheat-squares cereal or Necco wafers for roof shingles, and use starlight mints or M&M's around the edges to look like holiday lights . . . use your imagination and have fun!

24 DIY Gift: Design a set of personalized bookplates for your favorite bookworm! Bookplates are those cool stickers that go on the inside covers of books and say "This book is the property of (fill in the blank)." Most are about 3 × 4 inches in size. Make the plates by hand and decorate them with pressed flowers, stickers, glitter, ribbons, or magazine cutouts. If you don't have adhesive-backed paper, print them out on nice paper and include a glue stick in the package when you wrap them!

25 Gift wrap idea: Use your own artwork! Make a painting or a drawing and use it to wrap a small gift. Tie with a simple ribbon, and you'll have a truly one-of-a-kind package.

26 DIY Gift: Hairsticks! Paint a pair of chopsticks (ask for extras the next time you get Chinese takeout for dinner!). Paint them different colors, decorate with beads, markers, decoupage, small fabric flowers, and ribbon.

27 When packing a gift in a box, or packing a box that will be sent to someone via the mail, use plain air-popped popcorn as packing material. Be sure to use an air-popper for this—chances are excellent there's one at the back of your kitchen cupboard, or for cheap at your local thrift store—and don't add butter, salt, or any other seasonings to the popcorn. Not only is it inexpensive, but it's much better for the environment than commercial packing materials.

28 DIY Gift: Paint a set of four kitchen or bathroom tiles with funky shapes and flowers or decoupage them with pictures cut out of recipe magazines, put a sealing glaze on them, and tie them together with a ribbon for a nice set of coasters.

29 Simple, but beautiful holiday gift wrap idea: Wrap packages in plain brown paper (a cut up bag from the grocery store will work!) and tie pretty green, red, silver, blue, or gold ribbons around them.

30 DIY Gift: Flip through back issues of your favorite teen magazines and Web sites and choose 10–20 quizzes. Photocopy and print them out, make a cool cover, and staple together for a "personalized" teen mag for a friend.

31 Got gifts that don't fit your size or taste? Instead of returning them, consider donating your goods to a homeless shelter, children's charity, Goodwill, or other nonprofit group. Your castoffs could be another person's treasures, and vice versa! And what better way to end one year and begin the next than by sharing your gifts?

Resources and a Few More Ideas for DIY Inspiration!

You've Got Sale: Sources for Cheap and Chic Craft Supplies Online!

In addition to great craft store chains like Michaels, Hobby Lobby, Jo-Ann, and A.C. Moore, plus discount retailers like Target and Wal-Mart, drugstores, home improvement stores, and thrift shops, the Internet also provides plenty of great places where you can find DIY supplies, from the inexpensive to the truly unique crafty goods:

Jo-Ann.com *(www.joann.com)*—The online version of the national craft retailer, Jo-Ann.com has every kind of craft supply you can think of, and the site frequently offers great coupons, like 40 to 50 percent off online orders!

Save-On-Crafts.com *(www.save-on-crafts.com)*—This is one of the best craft-supply Web sites! Not only are the craft goodies cheap and plentiful, but they are arranged to help spark project ideas for you when you're browsing!

BlockheadsStamps.com *(www.blockheadstamps.com)*—Stamping supplies, glitters, micro beads, and other fun and unique paper craft supplies can be found at Blockheads. It's definitely the place to go for fun card-making supplies, and, in the site's cool "Gallery" section you'll find loads of project ideas!

Sei.com *(www.shopsei.com)*—This site offers cool scrapbook papers, including some amazing retro designs that can be used for dozens of crafts!

RibbonTex.com *(www.ribbontex.com)*—The number of projects you can make with pretty ribbons is limitless . . . but ribbon can also be fairly expensive. RibbonTex has a good variety, and even some of the most elaborate holiday and fabric ribbons are less than 15 cents a yard. Bargain!

M&JTrimming.com *(www.mjtrim.com)*—M&J is a famous New York City fabric trim store, where some of the world's most famous designers shop. Intricate beaded trims, embroidered ribbons, fancy buttons, and beautiful laces are just a few of the treasures to be found. And though the goodies aren't cheap, just one yard of a gorgeous fabric trim can truly turn a plain shirt or tote bag into a special piece that will look like you paid hundreds of dollars for it!

Reprodepot Fabrics.com *(www.reprodepotfabrics.com)*—the funkiest, grooviest fabric patterns ever, and the perfect materials for making cool pillows, tote bags, and other great gifts!

CreateForLess.com *(www.createforless.com)*—CFL is another general craft-supply Web site, but the selection is massive, the prices are good, and you get an extra discount if you buy in bulk, which, at CFL, means if you buy at least three of any one item. Good deal!

Now You're Cookin': Sources for Great Recipes Online!

Candies and cakes and cookies . . . oh my! You'll find recipes for all those goodies at these sites, as well as ideas for delicious drinks and savory sandwiches, and tips on making homemade versions of your favorite fast-food treats! Yum!

JustKidsRecipes.com *(www.justkidsrecipes.com)*—Recipes for Potato Pups, Rock Candy, and Chocolate Spiders are just a few of the freaky, but fun edibles available!

Allrecipes.com *(www.allrecipes.com)*—The name says it all . . . this Web site features more than 23,000 recipes, including suggestions for holiday foods, snacks, appetizers, entrees, drinks, and, of course, desserts!

Easy-Kids-Recipes.com *(www.easy-kids-recipes.com)*—You've never seen so many yummy recipes on one site, including casseroles, milkshakes, breakfast goodies, and even treats for your dog!

CookieRecipes.com *(http://cookie.allrecipes.com)*—If it's cookies you're in the mood for, you're sure to find the perfect recipe here!

CakeRecipe.com *(http://cake.allrecipes.com)*—No-bake cakes, cupcakes, ice cream cakes, coffee cakes, and even cakes you make from a box mix are among the more than 2,000 tasty treats at Cake Recipe.com!

About.com's Five-Ingredient Recipes *(http://busycooks.about. com)*—Click on the "Five Ingredients or Less" link to find hundreds of quick, easy recipes—including cookies, cakes, casseroles, breads, salads, and soups—that use less than five ingredients, but still manage to be incredible yummy!

TopSecretRecipes.com *(www.topsecretrecipes.com)*—This very cool site offers recipes for making homemade versions of your favorite restaurant foods! TSR includes recipes for whipping up your own version of Big Mac sauce, Cinnabon's Cinnastix, IHOP pancakes, Wendy's chili, the Starbucks Frappuccino, and even a homemade Reese's Peanut Butter Cup!

RazzleDazzleRecipes.com   *(www.razzledazzlerecipes.com)*— This site is full of recipes that are perfect for parties and holiday celebrations! It's the perfect excuse to have a sleepover or a party for your friends!